*A HOW*TO*BOOK*

The All-Occasion Craft & Gift Book

by Sally E. Stuart

 STANDARD PUBLISHING

CINCINNATI, OHIO

2138

DEDICATION

To all the teachers who shared their favorite ideas with me.

ISBN 0-87239-709-2

CONTENTS

INTRODUCTION

The ideas in this book are meant to supplement your classroom curriculum. They provide craft ideas that can be substituted when you wish to use a holiday or seasonal emphasis. Many of the ideas are for simple gifts that can be made for parents, friends, or shut-ins. Parents will find this a valuable resource for home craft projects.

In addition, you will find crafts related to specialty areas, such as missions, the Bible, and food—plus craft and gift ideas for any occasion.

Many of the ideas suggest variations or adaptations for different age levels. Although some are designated as preschool crafts, most do not have an assigned age. This has been done purposely, so you will not limit yourself in the use of this book. Most of the crafts can be simplified or expanded to fit any age group. You are encouraged to view each idea in light of your own pupils' interests and abilities, and adapt it accordingly.

All the ideas included in this book, even the major craft projects, are simple to make. Most call for ordinary supplies that are very accessible.

The General, Topical, and Craft Supply Indexes at the back of the book will help you in finding an appropriate craft idea quickly. Finding the right craft project, even at the last minute, will never be a problem again.

Winter

1

NEW YEAR'S IDEAS

CALENDAR NOTEBOOKS

Help pupils get ready for the new year by having them prepare their own combination calendar and diary.

Outline a plain calendar grid with squares large enough for a sentence, leaving space for a picture at the top. Duplicate it.

Give each child twelve of the calendar-grid pages (one for each month), two sheets of construction paper, and two or three brads. Have them make a book by putting the sheets between construction paper covers, and holding it together with the brads.

Provide an old calendar as a guide so they can name the months, number the days for each month, add an appropriate picture to each page, and decorate the front of their books.

The calendars will become personal dia-ries when they take them home and write in each square something special that happens that day. Plan a time *(perhaps right after Christmas)* when they can bring their calendars back to share with classmates.

Variation: You might want pupils to write in a good deed they accomplish each day, a Scripture verse they read, or some other activity to carry out a lesson they are learning.

NEW YEAR'S GOAL SETTING

For this activity, pupils will be preparing their own "time capsule." It will hold their goal for the coming months.

Cut out a quantity of four-inch squares *(or shape of your choice)* from colored construction paper. Give two to each child. Have him glue the two pieces together on three sides, leaving a pocket in the middle and one side open. Next, he may decorate his capsule any way he wishes, using crayons or cutout decorations.

When the capsule is completed, have him write on a slip of paper the thing he most wants to happen to him during the rest of this Sunday-school year. It can have to do with anything he wishes: a personal goal or accomplishment, something for his family, or whatever. Put the note inside the capsule and seal the opening. Be sure each one writes his name somewhere on the outside. Collect the finished "time capsules" and put them in a shoe box or other box of appropriate size. Wrap the box any way you wish and store it in a cupboard or on a shelf where students will see it and be reminded of their goals.

On your final Sunday together before the next new year, open the box and have students remove their capsules. Let those who wish share their goals and whether or not they were achieved.

Variation: If you wish, these goals could be linked to the thrust of your lessons for the coming months, or they could have to do with memorizing Scripture or spiritual goals.

SNOW ART

RAIN OR SNOW

Preschoolers will enjoy this simple handwork project on winter weather.

Give each child a sheet of blue construction paper which has been folded down the center. Print "Rain" at the top of one side, and print "Snow" at the top of the other side. The child may then use a black crayon to make "rain" on the appropriate side of his sheet. Add bits of cotton to the other side for snow. Put a few drops of glue at a time on each child's sheet, and let him stick a bit of cotton on each dot.

COTTONBALL SNOWMAN

Make this 3-D snowman on a 9 x 12 inch sheet of dark blue or black construction paper. Give each child three strips of white construction paper, 1 x 12 inches, 1 x 9 inches, and 1 x 6 inches. Make each strip into a ring by gluing the ends together. Stack the three rings, one above the other, to make the three sections of a snowman. Glue together at points of contact. Center the snowman shape on the background sheet. Stuff each section with cotton balls, putting white glue on the back of each ball first. Add a black construction paper hat and other features as desired to complete the picture.

WINTER JUNK ART

Ask pupils to bring in anything they can find that is white and that could be used in a junk-art snow picture. Suggest such things as white buttons, cotton swabs, cotton balls, cotton batting, white tissue paper, bath tissue, facial tissues, white plastic egg cartons, plastic packing material, straws, yarn, felt, fabric, etc.

Let each child select a variety of materials to make an all-white snow scene on a sheet of dark blue or black construction paper.

POPCORN SNOW

Before class, pop enough popcorn so each child will have his own full bowl. Let each one select a sheet of construction paper in the color of his choice. Squeeze out some white glue on a square of waxed paper. Have each child create a picture using the popcorn for anything he wishes: snowman and snow, fluffy clouds, flowers, buildings, animals, and people. Dip the back of each kernel in glue before adding it to the picture. Details can be added with colored chalk, crayon, tempera, or glued-on scraps of construction paper.

PLASTIC SNOWMEN

Peanut-shaped, plastic foam packing material can be used to create interesting snowmen. Give each child a sheet of dark-colored construction paper, and a quantity of the foam pieces. Instruct him to outline a snowman on his paper with a pencil, then fill in the outline with the foam pieces. The finishing features—hat, broom, buttons, etc.—can be cut from construction paper, felt, or fabric, and then glued in place.

The finished pictures can be used to decorate the room or put on a bulletin board. Add a memory verse and send them home to be displayed.

For younger children: Outline the snowmen on the sheets before distributing and give each child the remaining features all cut out and ready to glue in place.

SNOW SCENES

Add interest to the usual snow scene by using a variety of art methods. Give each child a sheet of grey construction paper and have him draw his scene, except for the snow, in crayon. Snow can then be added with white poster paint. *(He may wish to outline the areas to be painted with black or grey crayon first, for added emphasis.)*

MELTING SNOWMAN

This art project is in preparation for a memory-work activity.

Give each child a 9 x 12 inch or 12 x 18 inch sheet of white construction paper. Have him draw a large snowman with arms, a top hat, and any other features he wants. When completed, divide the snowman into the desired number of pieces, such as thirteen for each memory verse this quarter, or ten for each of the Commandments. Before class, you might determine how to best divide the snowman according to the number of parts needed: hat—1, head—2, middle—3, bottom—4, arms—2 each, etc.

Pupils can use a black crayon to mark off each section and number it. After putting his name in the last section, he may cut around the outline of his snowman, and add it to a prepared bulletin board.

As the child recites his memory verse each week, he cuts away the next section of his snowman, and watches him "melt" as he learns.

WOOLLY SNOW SCENE

Have the children draw a picture of their own church building on a sheet of blue construction paper, adding trees, shrubs, cars, houses, etc., around the building. When they are finished, they may add "snow" to their pictures by gluing on bits of white yarn. *(You will want to cut the yarn into tiny bits before class and give each child a handful.)*

Spread glue over a small section of the church roof and drop on bits of yarn to cover that section. Cover the entire roof, one section at a time. Then go on to add "snow" to the tops of trees, bushes, cars, etc.

GLITTERY SNOWFLAKES

Involve your pupils in making classroom decorations that may be left up through the winter months.

Cut eight-inch circles from sheets of heavyweight typing paper. Fold each circle in half, and then fold evenly into thirds *(forming a pie-shaped wedge).* Cut designs into the sides and wide end of the wedge, forming snowflakes. Remind the children, as they begin, that God made all snowflakes with six points and that no two are ever alike. Encourage them to be creative.

Have them open out the snowflakes and place on separate sheets of waxed paper. Carefully spread a thin layer of white glue over one side with fingers, and then sprinkle with silver glitter.

When the glue has dried, shake the excess glitter off onto the waxed paper and return it to a central container. Glue and glitter the back of each flake in the same manner.

Dry snowflakes may be suspended by lengths of thread from the ceiling, light fixtures, or in classroom windows.

WINTER DIORAMA

Give each child a 9 x 12 inch sheet of blue construction paper and have him draw a simple winter landscape scene. Be sure that the nine-inch edges form the sides of his picture.

When completed, give each child a 6 x 9 inch sheet of black construction paper. Mark off a one-inch border all the way around the edge. Then, with the nine-inch edges as the sides, have him draw a snowman on top of a mound of snow, using white chalk on the black paper. He may then use colored chalk to add features: buttons, hat, scarf, etc.

Next, cut around the shape of the snowman and mound, leaving it attached to the frame at the bottom. Continue to cut around the inside of the remainder of the one-inch frame.

Fold in a one-inch strip down both nine-inch sides of the landscape sheet. Apply glue to the folded strips and attach to the sides of the frame (curving the landscape scene behind the snowman).

FOR THE BIRDS

PINECONE BIRD TREAT

You will need a pinecone for each child, some inexpensive peanut butter, and a bag of birdseed. Before beginning, have them tie a piece of yarn around the top of the cone for hanging.

Have the children use craft sticks to coat their pinecones with peanut butter. After they are coated, roll them in birdseed. (Supply small, plastic sandwich bags as containers for carrying the cones home.) The cones may be hung in a tree or bush outside the house (near a window so they can watch the results).

NECKLACES FOR THE BIRDS

Ask the children to bring in stale, donut-shaped dry cereal, or any kind that has holes in it. Give each child a twelve-inch length of string and have him thread as much cereal on it as he can. Then tie the ends together to form a "necklace."

His bird "necklace" can be taken home to hang from a tree branch in his yard. If weather permits, you could take the children outside to hang their necklaces on a tree near their classroom window.

TREE FOR THE BIRDS

Get permission to "decorate" a tree on your church property as a bird-feeding station. If possible, select a tree that the children can see from their classroom window. Let each child select one or more of these "decorations" to make for their special tree.
Peanut-Butter Shells: Fill walnut shell halves with peanut butter, tie a piece of yarn around each, and make a loop on top for hanging.
Fruit Baskets: Scoop the fruit out of orange or grapefruit halves and cut the fruit into tiny pieces. Attach a string handle to each "basket" and fill with a mixture of apple and orange (or grapefruit) pieces (or bread crumbs).
Popcorn/Fruit Garlands: String plain popcorn, raisins, and cranberries on heavy thread with large needles. Drape over tree branches.
Fat Cones: Tie strings to the top of pine cones and stick small pieces of meat fat into cone openings.

Valentine's Day

2

LOVE AND HEART SCRIPTURES

Here are a number of Scripture verses which contain the word "love" or "heart." They can be used for Valentine related craft projects or activities.

Love: Deuteronomy 6:5
Psalm 18:1
Song of Solomon 2:4
Jeremiah 31:3b
John 13:35
John 14:23
John 15:12
John 15:13
Romans 8:28
Romans 8:35
Romans 12:10
Romans 13:8
1 Corinthians 13
Galatians 5:13, 14
Ephesians 6:24
Philippians 1:9
Colossians 3:14
1 Thessalonians 4:9b
Hebrews 13:1
1 John 2:15
1 John 3:1a
1 John 3:18
1 John 4:8

Heart: 1 Samuel 16:7
Psalm 26:2
Psalm 44:21b
Proverbs 3:5
Proverbs 10:8a
Proverbs 15:13
Proverbs 17:22b
Proverbs 22:15
Jeremiah 24:7
Ezekiel 18:31b
Matthew 11:29
Matthew 12:34b
Acts 1:24
Ephesians 6:6b

SUPER VALENTINE

To save your pupils the expense and trouble of purchasing valentine cards for each other, let them each make one SUPER valentine this year.

Outline a large heart on an 11 x 14 inch sheet of white construction paper for each pupil and have him cut it out. Then glue a three-inch red heart in the center of the white heart. He will write his name on the small heart.

When the valentines are completed, circulate them around the room and have each pupil sign his name or write a short note on each card.

For younger children: You cut out the hearts ahead of time and let the pupils glue the

11

small one in the center. Also give every child a quantity of small pink hearts, one for each child in the class. Have him print his name on each pink heart—or you do it for him. As the other children's hearts come around, he will glue one of his small pink hearts on it.

HEARTS TO YOU

Your pupils will feel better about themselves and each other after completing this variation of super valentines. *(See above.)*

Have each pupil prepare his valentine as described, but, when they are passed around, everyone is to write something nice about the owner of the card.

VALENTINE TRAY FAVORS

Your class might like to make valentine tray favors for a local hospital or nursing home. *(Be sure to check with them ahead of time to confirm your plans and to find out the correct quantity.)*

For each tray card, you will need a 4 x 6 inch, white unruled index card *(or white construction paper cut to the size),* and three one-inch red hearts. Fold the card the long way *(2 x 6 inches),* so it will stand up on the tray. On the left-hand side, glue on the three red hearts, slightly overlapping to form a bunch of flowers. Use a green crayon to draw a stem and leaves below each "blossom." Beside the bouquet, print an appropriate holiday message, such as: "Jesus Loves You" or "God Is Love."

VALENTINE COOKIES

Ahead of time, make two or more heart-shaped cookies for each child in your class. *(Be sure to bring several extras for visitors and to replace broken ones.)* Let pupils frost them with white frosting and decorate them as they wish with colored sprinkles, red sugar crystals, conversation-heart candies, coconut, etc.

Plan to eat one cookie in class. The others can be put in plastic wrap and taken home or given as a special valentine to a friend.

Variation: You may substitute plain, purchased sugar cookies and frost them with red frosting before adding decorations.

3-D VALENTINES

Collect a quantity of plastic lids from margarine tubs, chip cans, coffee or shortening cans, and the like. Cut circles of construction paper to fit inside each lid. Decorate each circle and print on an appropriate valentine greeting or Scripture verse. Glue the circle inside the lid. Spread glue around the outside edge of the lid and sprinkle with red glitter. Let dry. If desired, a hole can be punched in the top and a length of red yarn threaded through. Then the recipient can wear the valentine around his neck.

"JESUS LOVES YOU" CARD

Your pupils may want to make a special valentine for someone they know who is sick, in the hospital or a nursing home.

Cut out a quantity of double, red, construction paper hearts, with the fold on the left side so it can be opened. Give one to each child and have him glue the heart in the center of a white, paper doily. Glue a small picture of Jesus on the front and on the inside print: "Jesus Loves You."

For younger children: Have the words, "Jesus Loves You," already printed on small strips of paper so they can glue them inside their cards.

VALENTINE CADDY

If your pupils exchange valentines in class, you will want them to make this special heart to carry them home in.

Outline a nine-inch heart on red construction paper. Outline the lower five inches of the same heart on white construction paper. Have pupils cut out both pieces. Put the shapes together and glue or staple the outside edges, leaving a pocket where they can put their cards.

Let them decorate their heart any way they wish. Add a pink strip across the top of the pocket so they can print their name in large letters, or the words of a Scripture from the list provided at the beginning of this chapter.

CHEWY VALENTINES

Pupils can make special valentines for their friends or members of their family. Have them bring a stick of gum for each card they will be making.

Provide patterns for four-inch hearts, and let the children cut out a heart from red construction paper for each card. They can then glue a stick of chewing gum *(left in the wrapper)* to the center of each heart. Above and below the heart, print an appropriate message, such as: "I 'Chews' You for My Valentine" or "Stick With Me and I'll Stick With You."

VALENTINE FOR MOM

Here is a useful gift your pupils can make for their mother, grandmother, or favorite aunt.

Each child will need a medium-sized kitchen sponge *(new)* in a pretty color. *(These can be purchased at a variety or grocery store.)* You will also need a quantity of self-adhesive, valentine stickers.

Use a permanent black marker to print "Be My Valentine" *(or message desired)* in the middle of the sponge. Glue red rickrack or other trim around the edges. Decorate both sides with valentine seals.

After Valentine's Day, the decorations can easily be removed and the sponge used to wash dishes.

HEART ART

Cut out a large quantity of red, white, and pink construction paper hearts in one-, two-, three-, and four-inch sizes. Give each child a quantity of hearts in different colors and sizes, and a sheet of white construction paper. Let him use the hearts for the main parts of people, animals, and other objects to form a valentine picture or scene. He may use crayons to fill in any details needed in his picture, and glue to hold the hearts in place.

SCRIBBLE VALENTINE PUZZLES

Give each child a 9 x 12 inch piece of white construction paper or poster board, with a large heart outlined on it. He may cut out the heart first, or he can wait until he has decorated it. Using a black crayon, have him make a large "scribble" design all over the front of the valentine. Then he can use any color crayons he wishes to fill in the sections made by the overlapping lines of the scribble. When every section has been colored, the heart can be cut into several pieces and put into an envelope. It can be taken home to be enjoyed by the family, or given to a friend.

For younger children: Cut out the hearts and mark the cutting lines on the back for the child to follow. *(Make their hearts from construction paper so they will be easy to cut with small, blunt scissors.)* Mark each puzzle into only five or six simple pieces.

VALENTINE FOR PARENTS

A couple of weeks before Valentine's Day, take a picture of your class holding a sign that says: "Happy Valentine's Day! Can you find me?" Have a print made for each student to take home to his parents. Photos can be glued inside an appropriately decorated, construction-paper folder. Since the greeting is in the photograph, he need only sign his name underneath.

MACARONI HEARTS

Have pupils draw, freehand, three or four hearts in different sizes and shapes on a sheet of red construction paper or poster board. Provide three or four different types of macaroni, so pupils can fill in each heart shape with a different kind of macaroni, or mix the types within each heart. Across the bottom of the sheet, have them write the words of Proverbs 17:22: "A Merry Heart Doeth Good."

For younger children: Give each child a sheet of paper with one heart outlined. He will fill it in with one large type of macaroni. Have the Scripture written on a strip of paper so he can glue it on.

LOVE TREE

Paint a large, bare, tree branch with white enamel, and stand it upright in a bucket of sand. Have each pupil cut out one or more red hearts *(about three inches wide),* punch a hole in the top, and add a pink-yarn loop for hanging. Assign each pupil one or more verses *(from the beginning of this chapter).* Have him print the verse, or appropriate part of it, on his heart and hang from a tree limb. The tree can be used for the entire month of February, or longer if you like.

For younger children: Verses to be glued to the hearts can be printed or typed on small slips of paper.

PUNCHED HEARTS

Cut a four to six-inch heart from red poster board for each pupil. Have him punch holes *(using a paper punch)* evenly spaced *(about three-fourths inch apart)* all the way around the outside edge of the heart, being careful not to punch the holes too close to the edge. Give each one about a yard of white yarn to lace through the holes *(winding over the edge each time).* Tie the ends together in a bow at the top.

The valentines can then be completed as desired. Here are some ideas: (1) Glue his school picture in the center to give to a parent or grandparent. (2) Write an appropriate love verse. (3) Print a valentine greeting, such as: "Be Mine," "Be My Valentine," "Please Take My Heart," etc. (4) Glue on a small, purchased valentine. (5) Glue on a stick of gum or piece of wrapped valentine candy. (6) Glue on several conversation-heart candies.

SOMEONE LOVES YOU

This special valentine project will help remind your pupils of Jesus' love. Give each child a 9 x 12 inch sheet of red construction paper. Have him fold it in half, lengthwise, and cut out a large heart. *(You may wish to provide patterns.)* While still folded, make two cuts, about one-inch deep and two inches apart, to form the top and bottom of a window near the center of the heart. Cut on the fold line between the two slits. Fold back the flaps to form a window. Glue a picture of Jesus behind the window. Close the flaps. Have him print this caption above the window: "Open the Window to Find Someone Who Loves You." The hearts can then be decorated with crayons or trimmed as desired.

VALENTINE KITES

Decorate your classroom walls with special valentine kites made by your pupils. Give each pupil a kite shape outlined on an 11 x 14 inch sheet of red, white, or pink construction paper to cut out. Make kite tails from red or white crepe paper, cut into 1 and one-half inch strips. Staple the strips to the kites. Have the pupils print love Scriptures in the center of their kites. They can decorate with valentine stickers or by drawing on hearts, birds, butterflies—whatever they wish to carry out the valentine theme.

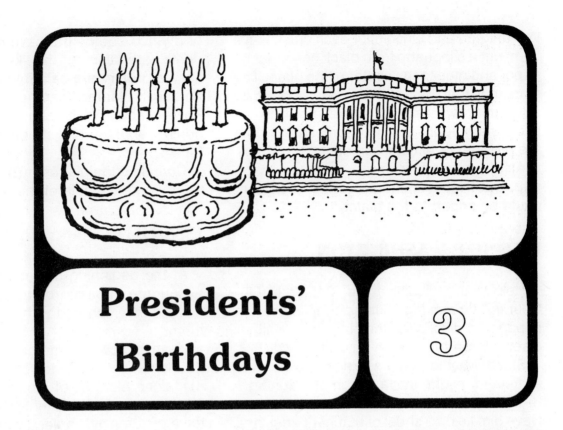

Presidents' Birthdays

3

PRESIDENTS AND ME

A common decoration for presidents born in February is the familiar black silhouette. Use these silhouettes for the center of your bulletin board, but let your pupils get into the act, too. Have the children help each other trace their own silhouettes, cut them from black construction paper, and add them to the bulletin board along with George and Abe.

To make the silhouettes, tape a sheet of white paper to the wall at the proper level. Set up a lamp opposite it, shining on the paper, and sit the child on a chair between the two to cast a shadow. Carefully outline the shape of his head on the paper. Cut it out and use as a pattern to cut a silhouette from black construction paper.

GEORGE'S HATCHET

Your pupils will enjoy making a "hatchet" to be used as a party favor or as a special craft project to commemorate George Washington's birthday. They may wish to make one for each member of their family, as a part of the family's celebration at home on the holiday.

You will need a cellophane-wrapped candy stick for the handle of each hatchet. Draw the outline of the head of a hatchet *(in proportion to "handle")* on colored construction paper, two outlines per hatchet.

Let the children cut out the two heads, place a candy stick between them, and glue the cutouts together at each side of the candy stick.

Note: You may wish to add a Scripture verse to the hatchet head, either on honesty or the memory verse for the day.

COMMEMORATIVE PLATES

Let pupils design a commemorative plate to honor one of the presidents. Provide a heavy paper plate and pattern silhouettes of

Washington and Lincoln for each child. Have them cut a silhouette from black construction paper and glue to the center of the plate. The plate may then be finished as they desire, by adding drawings, magazine pictures, or short statements that tell something about the president's accomplishments.

Also you might provide gummed stars, flags, patriotic stickers, glitter, etc., that could be added to the plates.

LIFE-SIZE WASHINGTON

Help pupils visualize the "Father of Our Country" by making a life-size replica of him in paper to display on the classroom wall, or elsewhere in the church for all to enjoy.

Since Washington was known to be over six feet in height, invite a man of that height to come to class and serve as a "model." Have him lie on a sheet of butcher paper, and let the pupils draw around him to form the basic outline for their "George."

Provide pictures of Washington, and let pupils fill in his features, hair, and clothing to match the pictures. He wore size 13 shoes, so try to borrow a pair of shoes that size. If they are not available, find out the approximate length and width and have someone make paper shoes of the proper size to be added to the bottom of the replica.

PRESIDENTIAL TRIPLETS

This triangular plaque is fun to make, calls for creativity from the pupils, and is a nice reminder of these famous presidents.

Gather together a number of small pictures of Lincoln and Washington, and perhaps other patriotic symbols, such as flags, the Liberty Bell, and the nation's Capital.

Each child will need three craft sticks. Have him glue the ends together to form a triangle. Then select a picture, trim it to fit, and glue it behind the triangle.

Next, have each child compose three lines of rhymed poetry that have to do with presidents, patriotism, or the like. These rhyming lines of poetry are called "triplets." They are unique in that they can be read in any order. For example: Washington was great. Lincoln could debate. Men shaping this country's fate.

Complete the plaque by writing one line of poetry on each side of the triangle.

LINCOLN PENNY CHART

At the beginning of February (or sooner), encourage pupils to bring in as many pennies as they can find with different dates on them.

Have them work together to prepare a 22 x 28 inch sheet of poster board by gluing on magazine pictures of Lincoln, collage style, to cover the whole sheet. Or, if you do not have pictures available, give each pupil a silhouette of Lincoln and have him draw on the hair and features, etc. Arrange these on the sheet.

When this is finished, have pupils sort their pennies, put them in order by dates, and mount them on the poster in even rows. Leave a space (outlined) for each date that is missing and write the date in that space. These may be filled in later if found.

For a caption, have someone write out a quote from Lincoln, or add an appropriate Scripture verse. Display the poster in your room for the rest of the month.

Variation: This activity could also be done with pictures of Washington and nickels, or combine both presidents on the same poster and use both pennies and nickels.

PAPER BAG PRESIDENTS

Involve your pupils in making paper bag puppets to represent both Washington and Lincoln, letting each pupil choose one or the other.

Each pupil will start with a lunch-size paper bag. He will draw on appropriate features, being sure the mouth is drawn where the bottom edge of the bag touches the side of the bag while folded.

Hang up some pictures of the presidents so the children will know what special features to add, such as a beard for Lincoln and a white wig for Washington. They also may want to add a black construction paper top hat to Lincoln.

Encourage them to copy a short quotation from Lincoln at the bottom of their bags, or write an original poem about him. Give each pupil the opportunity to show his puppet to the class. Let the puppet recite the quotation or poem in front of the group in a class or department program.

LINCOLN PENNY PUPPET

Provide a craft stick and a penny for each child. Have him glue the penny to one end of the stick to form the "head" of his puppet. He may then dress his puppet by adding black yarn for hair and beard and cutting a coat and hat from black felt or paper. Glue a toothpick flag in the puppet's hand.

Variation: The same project can be done for Washington by using a nickel or quarter for the head instead of a penny—and adding white cotton for hair, etc.

PRESIDENTS' PICTORIAL BIOGRAPHY

This project could honor either or both of our famous presidents. Provide books and pictures that depict the important events in the life of each president. Let each pupil pick out a different event *(or more than one if class is small)* and draw a picture to illustrate it.

Finished pictures could be hung on the wall in sequence, compiled into a book for another class, or presented in a special "President's Day" opening program for the church or department.

PRESIDENTS' MURAL

A variation of the previous project would be to have pupils prepare a mural of the important events in the life of each president. On a long sheet of butcher paper, mounted on the classroom wall, they could draw the events. They might like to prepare the mural as a comic strip, using stick figures.

"ABE" ROLL

These simple figures of Lincoln are fun to make and will stand up easily.

Each child will need a toilet tissue tube and a Styrofoam ball. Cover the tube with a strip of black construction paper cut to size. Glue the Styrofoam ball into place as the head. Features can be cut from construction paper or felt and glued or pinned in place. Add a yarn beard and hair. Top with a top hat made from black construction paper.

Variation: If Styrofoam balls are not available, have pupils cut heads from construction paper, glue them in place, and add features as above.

Spring

4

WISHING WELLS

These pretty wishing wells can be made to decorate your classroom, as a spring gift for mother, or as a service project to be taken to a local nursing home.

Have each child bring a half gallon milk carton from home. Using a craft knife, carefully cut a "window" in the top half of each side of the carton. Save the four panels and tape them together to form a roof for the wishing well, or cut a new roof from poster board. Glue into place on top of the carton.

Provide macaroni in various sizes and shapes so the pupils can decorate their cartons by gluing on the macaroni in a design of their choice, or covering it completely. When dry, the entire well can be spray painted in a spring color. Fill it with fresh flowers, or with dirt so a small plant can be planted.

Variation: Instead of real flowers or plants, make flowers by cutting blossoms from construction paper, writing a memory verse on each one, and stapling to drinking straw.

SPRING IDENTIFICATION

Spring is a wonderful time to emphasize and point out God's wonders. Take your class on a nature walk when the wild flowers are blooming in your area.

Have each child pick a different flower, leaf, or even weed to bring back. Avoid duplicates if possible. Next, have him mount the blossom or leaf on a piece of construction paper in a pastel color and print its name underneath. Provide some plant books to help with identification when needed. Display finished pictures.

Variation: If it is too difficult to discover the real names for the plants and weeds, let your students make up names for them according to their appearance. Discuss God's intricate planning that made each one different.

SPRING VASES OR FLOWERPOTS

A nice spring gift for mother or grandmother is a yarn-covered vase or flowerpot. Have each child bring from home an interesting shaped bottle *(such as salad dressing comes in)* or a plain flowerpot.

Starting at the bottom, brush on some white glue, covering only a small area at a time. Wind heavy yarn, string, or twine around and around the container, holding it in place until the first couple rows dry. Continue brushing on glue and winding until the container is completely covered.

When dry, add fresh flowers, dried flowers, or plants.

TISSUE PAPER FLOWERS

Let pupils work together to prepare classroom bouquets for spring, or have each one make his own bouquet to take home.

You will need cleansing tissues in a variety of pastel colors. Purchase boxes yourself, or assign each child a different color to bring. You will also need a green chenille wire for each flower. Follow these instructions to make fluffy, carnation-like flowers:

Use one whole tissue for each flower. Fold it in half and then into accordion pleats. Twist one end of the chenille wire very tightly around the center of the tissue. Cut the folded edge of the tissue open. Then gently pull the layers of the flower apart to form a fluffy blossom.

Variation: Cut green leaves from construction paper, write the day's memory verse on a leaf, and staple the leaf to the stem. Make a new flower with a new verse each week to add to the bouquet.

WIND CHIMES

Pupils can make these simple wind chimes and hang them outside their homes to catch the "music" of the spring winds.

Several weeks ahead, have pupils start saving cans of various sizes, including one the size of a forty-eight-ounce juice can. Each child will need four to six cans in addition to the large one. The large can will form the base.

Make holes, evenly spaced, around the open end of the large can, one for each of the smaller cans. Punch a hole in the center of each small can. Using various lengths of twine or heavy string, tie one end of each string to a hole in the large can. Then push the other end into the hole in a small can. Tie a large knot in the end of the string to keep it from pulling back through the hole in the small can. The cans should be hung at various levels, but they should all be able to touch one another when the wind blows.

Leave cans their natural silver color *(labels removed),* or paint them pretty colors before assembling. Decals may be added if desired.

SPRING GREETINGS

If time permits, let pupils make more than one of these pretty flowers to share with friends.

For each flower, they will need a small, pastel-colored paper plate, a green chenille wire, and a yellow yarn pom-pom.

Scallop the edges of the plate, glue the pom-pom in the center, and staple the green stem in place. Cut a leaf from green construction paper for each flower. Write "God Loves You" on the leaf and staple it to the stem.

These will make nice gifts for shut-ins or sick friends.

SEED POSTERS

As teachers, we want to remind our students constantly of the "wonder" in God's creation. A large seed poster will help our children recognize the overwhelming greatness of God even in the smallest seed.

Guide pupils as they prepare a poster to display a number of different seeds. Collect a variety of packets of seeds, or ask each child to bring a different type *(both flower and vegetable seeds).*

Caption a large sheet of poster board "Only God Can Make A Seed." Under the caption, have pupils glue the pictures from the front of the seed packets. Under each picture, using clear plastic tape, tape one or several of the tiny seeds from the packet.

Discuss the different sizes and shapes of the seeds displayed. Talk about how wonderful it is that the flower or vegetable can grow from such a tiny seed.

Variation: If you have enough pictures available *(seed catalogs are a good source),* let students make their own posters to take home.

3-D SPRING PICTURES

These spring pictures can be taken home and hung up as a reminder of God's goodness in giving us beautiful flowers, and even bees and bugs to help them grow.

Each child will need a Styrofoam meat tray *(or paper plate)* as a base for his picture. Have each pupil bring in a variety of trims such as lace, fringe, chenille wire, ball fringe, etc. Encourage them to use their trims and their imaginations to create interesting flowers, worms, butterflies, bees, bugs— even small animals to glue on their backgrounds.

After gluing everything in place, use felt-tip markers to add details. You also might want to supply tiny "eyes" that are available from craft stores. These can be glued to bugs and animals.

VARIEGATED BUTTERFLY

This multicolored butterfly is both beautiful to look at and fun to make. If you have only a short time for a craft project, it would be best to plan two or more sessions to complete it.

Each child will need a butterfly shape cut from white poster board. *(Approximate size: 11 inches from top to bottom of wing; 16 inches across widest top portion of wings; and 9 inches across bottom half of wings.)* Older children can trace their own butterflies if you provide patterns, or you can trace shapes on pastel-colored poster boards and let them cut them out. For younger children, cut out shapes before class.

Provide a large quantity in a variety of bright colors of one and one-half—two-inch squares cut from tissue paper. Each child will need a pencil and a small lid or container of white glue. Pick up a single square of tissue, wrap it over the eraser end of the pencil, dip the tip in glue, and press it into place on the butterfly with the pencil. Gently hold the tissue in place as you remove the pencil. Repeat with the next piece of tissue. Continue adding these "tufts" of tissue until the entire butterfly shape is solidly covered. Add black, chenille-wire feelers, if desired.

PAPER DAFFODIL

The day's memory verse can be written on the bottom of a 9 x 12 inch sheet of brightly colored construction paper. Let the children add a pretty daffodil to their sheet as a reminder of spring.

Trace three and one-fourth inch long daffodil petals on yellow construction paper *(six per pupil).* Have the children cut them out. Next, have them glue the petals in a circle on the top half of their background sheet. In the center where the petals join, glue a yellow nut cup or small, yellow cupcake liner. Draw on the stem and leaves with a green felt-tip marker or crayon.

PUSSY WILLOW CREATURES

When spring starts showing its head, it will be time to remind your pupils to look for pussy willows. Encourage them to bring some to class to use in this spring project.

Give each child a sheet of construction paper and have him glue a "fuzzy" onto it. Using that as a body, he can add a head, legs, tail, etc., to make it into an animal of his choice. He may want to go on and create an entire picture, using a "fuzzy" for each person, animal, or anything else he can come up with.

Variation: Use this idea to make greeting cards, or to make place cards to go on hospital or nursing home dinner trays.

PAPER PLATE LAMB

This lamb is fun to make for spring, or anytime you are studying about the good shepherd or similar lesson.

Each pupil will need a white paper plate and several cotton balls. Provide white construction paper or poster board cut in the shape of ears to staple in place on each side of the "head." Cut a mouth and eyes from construction paper and glue into place. Add a cotton ball for the nose. Glue a row of cotton balls across the top of the head between the ears. Additional features may be added with crayons or felt-tip pens.

SCRIPTURE RAINDROPS

Big spring raindrops with Scripture verses added will brighten up your classroom.

Supply several patterns for eighteen-inch raindrops. Have a sheet of light blue 12 x 18 inch construction paper for each child. Let him trace a raindrop on his sheet and cut it out. *(Have them already cut out for younger children.)*

Next, have each child select a Scripture verse that deals with nature. Let him write the verse on one side of the raindrop. On the other side, he may draw a picture to illustrate the verse or to illustrate spring.

Punch a hole at the top of each raindrop and hang it from the ceiling or a light fixture.

SPRING MURAL

This project can be carried out over two or three weeks if you like. Before class the first week, tape up an eight-foot piece of butcher paper. Glue a large picture of Jesus in the center. Bring to class a large collection of pictures of children, cut from magazines or catalogs. Also provide a quantity of gummed or self-adhesive flower and bird seals.

Have the children begin by coloring a border of grass along the bottom of the mural. Older children can add a sun, trees, and rocks to the picture. Then have the students glue the children in place, covering the full length of the mural. Finally, add the flower seals to the grass *(draw on stems and leaves if needed)* and the birds flying in the sky.

PRESCHOOL CRAFTS

The following are a variety of very simple spring crafts for use with young children.

CLOTHESPIN BUTTERFLY

Each child will need a white or pastel-colored napkin and an old-fashioned *(non-clipping)* clothespin. Let each child color and decorate his napkin as he wishes. Then he can insert it in the opening of the clothespin to form the wings of his butterfly. He may wish to add eyes to the head of his butterfly.

WOOLLY SHEEP

Give each child a 3 x 5 index card *(in a pastel color if possible),* and two or three cotton balls. Have him glue the balls to the card *(leaving space between them).* Use a black crayon to add legs, a head, and ears to make each ball into a soft lamb.

STAND-UP GARDEN

For each child you will need a sheet of brown construction paper, folded in half, an orange crayon, and several small strips of green construction paper.

Have the child draw three or four carrots on his paper, with the top of each carrot on the fold line *(the fold represents the top of the ground)*. Glue three small strips of green paper to the top of each carrot so it extends above the fold.

Write the day's memory verse under the carrots. The child can take home his "stand-up" garden.

BIRD NEST

Provide a bottle cap and a quantity of green yarn for each pupil. Cut yarn into tiny bits *(or use bits of green crepe paper)*. The child puts a dab of glue inside the bottle cap, and then adds the bits of yarn or paper to make a "nest." Give him a small plastic bird, or one cut from construction paper, to add to his nest.

BUTTON TURTLE

Cut a turtle shape from brightly colored construction paper or poster board—one for each child. Supply a large quantity of buttons. Ask the children to bring some from home if necessary.

Children select buttons and glue them in place to cover the turtle's shell completely.

EGG CARTON CATERPILLAR

Make caterpillars from one long side of an egg carton. Poke two holes in the first egg cup, fold a chenille wire in half, and stick one end through each hole for an antenna. Let the children paint and decorate the bodies as they please.

BUBBLE BLOWING

On a sunny spring day, take your little ones outside to blow bubbles. Here is a recipe that makes big bubbles.

Mix in a large jar: 2 cups water
$\frac{1}{4}$ cup liquid glycerin *(available at the drug store)*
2 teaspoons liquid detergent

Plastic straws can be used for blowing bubbles. Have the children dip one end in the bubble mixture, remove, and then blow through the other end.

FLUTTERY BUTTERFLY

For each child you will need a butterfly shape cut from construction paper and a drinking straw. Let each child decorate his butterfly shape with sequins, glitter, or small pieces of multicolored construction paper glued on at random. When the decorations are dry, staple the butterfly to one end of the drinking straw. The child can hold the free end of the straw and "flutter" his butterfly.

Palm Sunday and Easter

5

EASTER CALENDAR

You will find accounts of Jesus' last days, from Passover to resurrection, in these passages of Scripture:

Matthew 26:17 through Matthew 28:20
Mark 14:12 through Mark 16:20
Luke 22:7 through Luke 24:53
John 13:1 through Acts 1:11

A brief calendar of His last week is as follows:

*Palm Sunday—Triumphal entry into Jerusalem and teaching in the temple.

*Monday—Chased money changers from temple.

*Tuesday—Went to the temple for the last time, ending His public ministry.

*Wednesday—Judas made plans to betray Jesus. Jesus was probably in or near Bethany.

*Thursday—The last supper. Jesus prayed in the Garden of Gethsemane and was then arrested by the soldiers.

*Friday—Taken before Annas and Caiaphas during the night, before the Sanhedrin before daylight, and before Pilate about dawn. Went before Herod, returned to Pilate and was sentenced. Crucified and died about 3 P.M. Buried before sundown.

*Saturday—Jewish Sabbath. Guards watched tomb.

*Sunday—Jesus arose!

CLAY PRETZELS

Share with your pupils that pretzels are a food that was used by early Christians. The shape of the pretzel represents two arms crossed in prayer. Bring samples for your students to look at *(and eat later)*.

Using the purchased pretzels as a pattern, have pupils roll out their own pretzels from clay. You might want to make them from a salt and flour dough that can be dried and then painted as a lasting Easter momento for each child.

EASTER CROSSES

Before class, light and extinguish a large quantity of wooden matches. *(Each pupil will need two to three dozen.)*

Give each pupil a sheet of waxed paper to work on, to keep his design from sticking. Each one will arrange his matches in the shape of a cross and glue them together. You might provide single-edge razor blades for teen pupils to cut their matches to different lengths. Cut them for younger children. Encourage them to use their imaginations to create some unusual designs in their crosses.

EGGHEAD STORY FIGURES

Make egghead figures to illustrate the Easter story. For each character, you will need a blown-out eggshell and a cardboard, toilet-tissue core. Glue the eggshell on top of the tube. Draw on a face with permanent felt markers. Dress each character appropriately, with construction paper arms and clothing, yarn hair and beards, fabric headpieces, etc. You will need all the main characters for the story, plus people to be part of the crowd *(if you have too many pupils or some wish to make more than one figure)*. To save confusion, you might have pupils draw names for the characters they will create.

EASTER "BASKETS"

Individual, Styrofoam boxes that fast-food restaurants use for hamburgers make unique Easter baskets. These can be saved up or purchased from a local restaurant.

Collect a quantity of Easter pictures or pictures of Jesus that can be cut to fit the inside of the lid. You may want to provide patterns so pupils can cut pictures to the correct sizes. Glue in place. Put Easter grass in the bottom half and add Easter candy, decorated eggs, or cookies. Add a gold cross sticker to

the center on the outside of each lid. The baskets could be made a week ahead, and the contents *(eggs or cookies)* made on Easter Sunday.

ILLUSTRATED EASTER SONGS

Select one of your pupils' favorite Easter songs that will lend itself to illustrating. Divide the song into lines or parts, so each child *(or two children together)* can be assigned a part. Give every child *(or couple)* an 11 x 14 inch sheet of white construction paper on which you have neatly printed along the bottom his assigned words from the song. Let him draw an appropriate illustration for his part of the song. Completed sheets can be fastened to the wall or held up, in order, as the children sing the song together. Take the drawings and sing your song for other classes—or even teach it to them.

EASTER DINNER NAPKINS

Help your pupils make a contribution to the family's Easter dinner. Provide enough pastel-colored napkins so each child will have one for every member of his family. Bring a variety of Easter-related stickers, such as flowers, crosses, Jesus, etc. Let the children put a sticker in the corner of each napkin, roll it up, and tie it with a length of ribbon. If desired, pupils can make name tags. On one-inch strips, cut from white index cards, write a name, punch a hole in one end, and tie it onto the ribbon.

For younger children: Let them put on the stickers. Then you roll the napkins, tie them, and add name tags.

EASTER BELLS

Have your pupils make bells to use in accompanying your Easter songs. Let them take the bells home as a reminder of this happy occasion.

For each bell, you will need a Styrofoam or paper cup, a short, white shoelace, and a small bell. Make a hole in the bottom of the cup with a large nail. Thread the bell onto the shoelace and push it to the center. From inside the cup, push the ends of the shoelace through the hole, and tie into a bow on the outside. *(The bell will stay inside the cup.)* Let pupils decorate their cups with crayons, felt-tip markers, or cut out paper decorations. Glue on a construction paper strip with the words "Sing for Jesus," or other appropriate message.

PALM LEAVES

Preschoolers will be able to make these simple palm leaves to wave as they listen to the story of Jesus' entrance into Jerusalem. Then let them sing a favorite Easter song.

Give each child half of an 11 x 14 inch sheet of green construction paper, which you have folded lengthwise. Using blunt scissors, each child can cut snips along both long sides, being careful not to cut all the way to the fold.

EASTER EGG COOKIES

Pupils can decorate egg-shaped cookies by painting them with food-color "paints" before baking.

Before class, mix up your favorite rolled cookie dough. *(Chill if needed.)* When ready, roll out dough and cut egg shapes with a cookie cutter *(or cut around a cardboard pattern).* Mix up "paints" by adding one teaspoon water and a few drops of food coloring to an egg yolk for each color desired. Supply clean paintbrushes. Let a few work at a time to decorate their cookies to resemble Easter eggs.

A helper or mother can bake them in the church kitchen. Have her return them to class in time to eat, put in prepared Easter baskets, take home, share with other classes or give away.

MR. EGGHEAD PLANTER

For each child you will need an eggshell that has been cracked open close to one end. *(Save only the large part of the eggshell. Rinse out and let dry.)*

Each pupil will use felt-tip markers to make a face on his eggshell, open end up. From construction paper, he will make a collar on which to stand his egg. Decorate the collar appropriately with the felt-tip markers or glued-on construction paper pieces. Staple together at the back.

When completed, carefully fill the egg with dirt and grass seed. Water sparingly. When the grass grows, Mr. Egghead will have a full head of "hair."

EASTER MOBILE

After a discussion of the various symbols associated with the Easter season, have your pupils work together to make one or more Easter mobiles as a class decoration *(or one each to take home).* Provide a quantity of appropriate pictures, such as palm leaves, lilies, crosses, Communion emblems, butterflies, sunrises, lambs, Jesus, tombs, etc. You will need two pictures of each symbol, to be glued back to back. You may wish to have them put a piece of construction paper, cut to the right size, between the two pictures. Cut pieces of string to different lengths. Attach one end of a string to the picture, and tie the other end to a wire coat hanger.

HATCHING CHICKS

Hatching chicks can represent new life and the resurrection of Jesus to your pupils.

Have pupils cut out two identical egg shapes, free hand or using patterns you provide. Next, cut a jagged "crack" across the middle *(top to bottom)* of one of the egg shapes. Fit the two halves back together and lay on top of the whole egg shape. When they are lined up, put a paper fastener close to each end of the egg, to hold the two egg shapes together. When the top pieces are swung out to the sides, they become the wings of the chick. Next, cut out separate pieces for the head and two legs. Attach these with paper fasteners to the whole egg shape. When the head and legs are turned to the inside, and the wings turned back to hide them all, it looks like an egg again. Add finishing features, as desired, with crayons.

EASTER CROSSES

Bring to class a supply of small sticks, plastic lids from aerosol cans, clay, and small spring flowers *(real, dry, or artificial)*. Have pupils use string or heavy thread to tie two sticks together to form a cross. The horizontal stick will need to be shorter than the vertical one. Put clay in the small hole in the center of the lid. Stand the cross up in the clay. Stick flowers into the clay around the base of the cross. These can be taken home as a family gift.

BUNNY BAGS

These inexpensive containers can be made by your pupils to share with the children in a children's home or hospital. For each bunny bag, you will need a small paper bag, plus some felt-tip markers, scissors, and stapler.

Provide patterns for pupils to use in cutting a "U" shape from the top center of each bag. Cut through both thicknesses, about halfway down the length of the bag, but leave room on each side of the "U" for the bunny's ears. Use the markers to draw on features for the bunny's face and to outline the ears on each side of the cut. *(Ears should not come all the way to the top edge of the bag.)* Overlap the ends and staple together above the ear tips. The bags can then be filled with Easter grass, jelly beans or other Easter candy, and an Easter tract or picture.

JELLY BEAN TREE

Plant a bare tree branch in a bucket of sand. Decorate the tree with strings of jelly beans, paper birds, and butterflies. Have some pupils cut out the birds and butterflies from different colors of construction paper, using patterns provided. Others can use a large needle and thread to string jelly beans together. *(Oversized jelly beans work better.)* Two to six jelly beans strung together on the same piece of thread can be tied to a tree branch. Let the jelly beans hang down. Attach a thread to each paper bird and butterfly, and tie these to the branches also. The tree should be filled full to make an attractive room decoration for Easter and spring.

EASTER SERVICE PROJECT

Your pupils will enjoy this Easter service project for shut-ins. They will need to dye and decorate four eggs for each person or couple. To make baskets, cut the bottom halves of egg cartons into three sections. Give each child a four-cup section to color or decorate as he wishes. Punch a small hole in each side of the "basket." Add a handle with a pretty color of chenille wire. Put a little Easter grass and a decorated egg in each section, and they will be ready to deliver.

EASTER BASKET COOKIES

These special cookies resemble miniature Easter baskets. Each child will need one or two large sugar cookies *(homemade or purchased)*. Provide white frosting, green tinted coconut, and jelly beans. *(To tint coconut, put it in a jar with a few drops of green food coloring and a little water. Shake until evenly colored.)* Have the children frost their cookies, sprinkle with green coconut, and dot with jelly beans. Let them eat one cookie in class, but take the extra one *(wrapped in plastic wrap)*, along with an Easter tract, to share with a friend.

Mother's Day 9

CARDS

PAPER CUP CARD

Each child will need a 7 x 9 inch sheet of construction paper, in a pretty pastel color, and a pastel-colored paper bake cup.

Fold paper in half to make a 3½ x 9 inch card. Flatten the paper bake cup, fold it in half, and then in half again to make the blossom for the flower. Glue it in place *(open end up)* at the top front of the card. Cut a calyx from green construction paper and glue in lace to cover the lower point of the blossom. With green crayon, draw on a stem and leaves. Print "To My Mother" at the bottom. Add a Mother's Day message inside.

"THANKS, MOM" CARD

Fold an 8 x 9 inch sheet of construction paper in half to make a long, narrow card. Have pupils draw small pictures or cut them from magazines to show some of the things mother does for them. Print "Thanks, Mom, For:" at the top on the front of the card. Then glue on the small pictures with an appropriate caption next to each, such as: ironing my clothes, fixing good meals, baking my favorite cookies, etc. Continue the list on the inside of the card. Sign it.

POEM CARD

Duplicate the following poem *(or one of your choice)*. Have pupils glue it inside a construction paper card *(a 9 x 12 inch sheet folded in half)*.

Mother loves me! This I know,
For she always tells me so.
She cares for me everyday
And even finds time to play.

Gather together a variety of trims, gummed seals, and tiny dried flowers. Let the children use these to decorate the fronts of their cards as they wish.

FINGERPRINT CARDS

Bring to class one or more ink pads (in different colors, if possible). Have pupils fold a sheet of construction paper for a card. Then put several of their fingerprints in a random arrangement on the front of the card, pressing their fingers on ink pad and then onto the paper. Using the fingerprint as the head or body of an animal or person, have them add details with a black, felt-tip pen. They may wish to practice on a piece of scratch paper first.

Add a personal message inside the card.

PRESCHOOL IDEAS

"I LOVE MY MOTHER" CARD

Prepare a construction paper card for each child. Let him decorate the front as he pleases.

Individually, ask each child why he loves his mother, and then write his answer inside the card. "I love my mother because . . ." This message will mean a lot to each mother.

Note: If your class is large, you might like to enlist some extra helpers to write down the messages.

HANDPRINT CARD

Each child will need a half sheet of brightly-colored construction paper. Write his name on the back. Provide materials so the child can put a border around the edges of his card. Borders can be made from glue and glitter, rickrack, sequins, lace, braid, or other trims.

When the border is complete, print, "I Will Be Your Helper, Mommy" at the bottom of the card. Outline the child's handprint in the center of the card.

Be sure the child understands what the message on the card says—and agrees to it. Discuss ways he might help.

FLOWER PICTURE

Sometime before Mother's Day, take pictures of your pupils (2 or 3 together against a plain background). Cut the picture apart, separating the children.

Give each child a sheet of construction paper with "To the Special Mother God Gave Me" printed down the side of the sheet. Have the child glue the flat bottom of a pastel-colored paper bake cup near the top of the sheet. Next, he may add a stem and leaves with green crayon. Cut each child's picture to fit inside the bake cup. Have him glue it in place.

HANDPRINT PLAQUE

This handprint plaque will be a special gift for mother that the children will enjoy making.

Each child will need a brightly colored 9 x 12 inch sheet of construction paper, and a dark-colored 6 x 9 inch sheet. For each six to eight handprints, beat together one cup of soap flakes and one-third cup water to the consistency of thick whipped cream.

Before proceeding with the spatter method below, the child should put on a paint shirt or other covering to protect his good clothing.

Have the child place his hand, fingers spread apart, on the small sheet of construction paper. Dip a stiff brush in the soapsuds. Use your fingers to scrape the suds off, as in spatter painting. Make the soapsuds thickest around the outside of his hand. Carefully lift the child's hand from the paper, and set the print aside to dry.

When prints are dry, glue each one to a larger sheet of construction paper. Punch two holes at the top and add a ribbon bow. Under the print, glue a special Mother's Day poem or message, or an appropriate Scripture verse.

GIFTS

HELPING BOXES

This idea expands on the usual job offers for Mother's Day.

Each pupil will need five squares of construction paper in one color, and five more in a second color. On each of the first five squares, he should write a different task he might do for his mother around the house, such as: washing dishes, taking out the trash, dusting, etc.

On the second five squares he will write something he would like his mother to help him with, such as: help with homework, a lesson in sewing, a ride to the park, etc.

Each child will decorate a small box (supply or have children bring from home) and place all ten squares inside.

During the next five days, both mother and child will draw a slip of the proper color and do what it suggests.

Variation: This idea can be changed from "Helping Boxes" to "I Love You Boxes" by having the child write a message of love or appreciation on each slip.

POMANDER

Making an old-fashioned pomander will be a project your children will enjoy, and their mothers will love receiving. Be sure to start four to six weeks before Mother's Day.

Each child will need a small, firm, thin-skinned orange, apple, or lemon, and enough whole cloves to cover it completely (three ounces should cover two small oranges). Remind the children to use only cloves with the heads on.

If cloves won't push in easily, make holes first with a small nail. When fruit is completely covered, roll it in a mixture of ground cloves, cinnamon, ginger, nutmeg, and allspice.

Carefully wrap the ball in a square of brightly colored nylon net, tie it with a ribbon, and leave a loop at the top to hang it up. The ball should hang in a warm, dry spot for four to six weeks to cure. During this time, the skin will shrink and will no longer show between the cloves.

LETTER HOLDER

Give each child one whole and one half paper plate. Punch holes, evenly spaced, around the outside edges of each. Be sure the holes in the two pieces line up. Lay the half plate on top of the whole one, fronts together. Lace them together with yarn or a bright shoestring. Tie ends in a bow at the top.

Decorate plates with poster paint or self-adhesive stickers. Add a yarn hanger at the top, and paint Letters, Mail, or Notes across the front of the half plate.

GIFT POSTCARDS

For an unusual gift, let pupils make their mothers a set of custom-made postcards.

Each child will need six, 4 x 6 inch, unruled cards in a pretty color. On one side of each card, have pupils use a ruler to divide the card in half with a vertical line. Also draw three horizontal lines on the right-hand side for the address. Draw a small square in the upper, right-hand corner of the card. Print "Stamp" in the square and "Postcard" next to the box, if desired. Leave the left-hand side of the card blank for the message.

The fronts of each card can then be decorated in any way the pupil wishes. He might use painted or colored designs or pictures, pictures appropriate to mother's interests, funny captions, poems, or carefully-selected magazine pictures. He should sign his own name to the lower, right-hand corner of his design, as an artist would.

Tie completed cards together with a ribbon and add a Mother's Day greeting.

GOLD VASE

Each child will need to select his own glass, jar, or bottle. The more unusual the shape, the prettier the vase.

Several weeks before doing this project, start saving eggshells, and ask your pupils to do the same. Shells should be rinsed, membrane removed, and then dried. Break the dried shells into tiny pieces.

Containers must be covered liberally with white glue. Then roll them in the crushed eggshells to cover completely. When the glue is dry, spray the shell-covered container with gold paint to make a lovely vase for a Mother's Day gift.

SEWING KIT

Here is a different idea for a sewing kit that Mother can carry in her purse or suitcase.

Each child will need a metal aspirin tin. Paint it with a bright-colored enamel, and let it dry. Decorate the top with a self-adhesive sticker.

Next, have the child cut a piece of cardboard to fit inside the tin *(provide patterns)*. Cut two small slits on one side of it. Wrap the cardboard with both black and white thread. Use the slits to anchor the loose ends. Slip one or two needles under the thread, and add two or three small safety pins to the box.

RIBBON BOOKMARK

If you need a quick, inexpensive gift for your children to make for Mother's Day, this bookmark will be it.

For each bookmark, you will need a 2 x 5 inch strip of construction paper. Using a hole punch, punch three rows of holes the length of the strip *(about six holes per row and staggered unevenly)*.

Give each child three strips of ribbon or rug yarn. Weave one piece through the holes in each row. Put a dab of glue at the end of each row to hold the ribbon or yarn in place. The pieces of ribbon or yarn need to be long enough to trim away any frayed ends and still have enough length to hang over each end of the bookmark.

PICTURE TRAY

You may need to plan several Sundays to work on this serving tray for mother.

Have each child bring a small, inexpensive tray to class, or you may wish to buy a quantity of them.

Bring a supply of magazines, take-home papers, or calendars from which pupils can cut pictures. Before they begin, they should decide on a theme, such as: flowers, cats, dogs, trees, butterflies, birds, or mother's special interest. Have them cut out appropriate pictures, trim away any excess border, and glue on the tray. Cover it completely, collage style. Be sure all corners are glued down neatly. When the glue is dry, cover with a coat of clear shellac. Dry thoroughly and add a second coat.

RECIPE ORGANIZER

Every mother will appreciate this organizer.

For each one, you will need eight 9 x 12 inch manila envelopes, and three loose-leaf book rings.

Have pupils label each of their envelopes. Find a magazine picture to illustrate the type of food indicated and glue it to the front of the envelope. Envelopes may be labeled: Main Dishes, Salads, Vegetables, Cookies, Cakes, Desserts, Breakfast, and Household Tips.

Use a three-hole punch to put holes along the left-hand side of each envelope. Be sure the holes on each envelope line up. Also punch holes in two sheets of poster board (9½ x 12½ inches) for covers. Print Recipe Organizer on the front cover. Decorate with small pictures of food cut from magazines and glued on.

Father's Day

7

CARDS

"FATHER IS . . ." CARD

Give your pupils the opportunity to come up with some original Father's day greetings for this card for dad.

Before starting, write "A father is . . ." at the top of your chalkboard. Ask pupils to give you as many answers as they can. Write them all on the board.

Give each pupil a 9 x 12 inch sheet of construction paper. Have him fold it any way he wishes to make a card. Let him select his favorite message off the board and print it inside the card.

Decorate the front of the card, reflecting the message inside, if possible.

SAILBOAT CARD

Have each child bring a new, white man's handkerchief to class, or you provide them.

Give each one a 9 x 12 inch sheet of blue construction paper. Have him fold it in half and outline a simple sailboat, with a mast, on the front. Print Happy Father's Day across the bottom, under the boat. Draw in a simple sail and cut a slit at the top and bottom of the sail. Fold the handkerchief the same width as the slits, and slip the ends into the slits so the handkerchief forms the sail. The ends will be inside the card. Glue the outside edges of the card together, enclosing the ends of the handkerchief.

STUFFED SHIRT CARD

This unique card will remind Dad how much he is loved this Father's Day, and the children will enjoy making a card that looks like a man's dress shirt.

Give each child a sheet of white drawing paper, 4½ x 11 inches. Have him fold it across the middle with the fold at the top of the card. Make a small pencil mark one inch down from the fold on each side of the card. Starting at the pencil mark, make a one-inch slash on each side of the card, slanting it slightly upward to make the shape of the shoulders. Fold the portions above the slashes toward the center to form the collar of the shirt. Cut a necktie and handkerchief from a sheet of print wrapping paper or wallpaper in an appropriate design. Glue the necktie in place, and then glue down the collar over the tie. Use a felt-tip marker to draw on a pocket and buttons. Glue the handkerchief to the top of the shirt pocket.

Add a suitable message inside, such as: "This Shirt Is Stuffed With Lots of Love for My Dad."

LIFE-SIZE GREETING

For these oversized Father's Day greetings, you will need a roll of white paper (like is used to cover tables) or end rolls of newsprint available from a local newspaper office.

For each child, cut a length of paper the child's height, plus a few inches. Have the child lay on the paper while a partner or classroom helper draws around the outline of his body. The child will then color in the hair, features, and clothing to match his own. When completed, have him print "My Name Is _____" at the top of his portrait and "I Love My Dad" at the bottom. Roll up and tie with a ribbon.

PRESCHOOL IDEAS

JESUS BOOKMARK

This gift bookmark will remind dad of his toddler's love and God's love.

Before class, prepare 2½ x 6 inch bookmarks cut from brightly colored construction paper. Along the center print the words, "God Gave Me My Daddy."

In class, let each child add a gummed sticker of Jesus at the top of the bookmark. Then help him sign his name at the bottom.

DESK ORGANIZER

Collect a quantity of colored foam egg cartons. Cut them into four-cup sections. Each child will need one of these four-cup sections. (If foam cartons are not available, spray paint the pressed paper ones or cover them with foil.)

Let the children put paper clips in one section, a small eraser in one, thumbtacks in one, and rubber bands in the last one. Cover with clear plastic to keep the contents from spilling. Tie with a bow.

WIGGLY WORM BOOKMARK

From colored paper, cut a quantity of circles in four different sizes (1¼", 1⅛", 1", and ⅞"). Use nine circles for each worm. Give each child one of the largest circles and have him draw a face on it. He will also need two of the one and one-eighth-inch circles, and three each of the other two sizes. Lay them out in the order they will be added to the worm (graduated, largest to smallest), but don't worry if a child mixes them up.

Let each child put a small dab of glue or paste on the front edge of each circle and slip it under the circle before it. The circles can be added in a straight line or in a wiggly one to make a "wiggly" worm.

CROWN CARD

You will need a snapshot of each child. Obtain them from parents, or take your own ahead of time in class.

The base for each card should be cut from construction paper, ahead of time, in the shape of a simple crown. Leave the center of the card blank to make room for the picture. On each side of the space print, "To Dad— King of Our Home."

Have each child glue his picture in place. If desired, print a Bible verse under the photograph.

GIFTS

MARBLE PEN HOLDER

This project will require a large quantity of marbles, some felt, white glue, and a desk-type pen for each holder.

Provide a pattern for students to use to cut a triangle from felt. *(The triangle should measure about four inches on each side.)* Work with the felt on a piece of waxed paper on a flat surface, and cover the triangle completely by gluing marbles on in even rows. Let dry before going on.

Next, glue another layer of marbles on top, fitting them between the marbles on the first layer. Let dry.

Roll a piece of foil around the end of the pen and tape to hold. Remove the pen. Place the foil in the marbles at a slant to form an open hole to insert the pen in later. Holding the foil in place, continue building the pyramid of marbles. *(Let each row dry before going on to the next.)* You will complete the pyramid with one marble on top. When it is completely dry, remove the foil tube and slip the pen into the hole.

MR. EGGHEAD

Your pupils will need to start these unusual plants a few weeks before Father's Day.

Each pupil will need an empty eggshell with the top portion of one end broken away. Give each one a three-inch square of cardboard and have him cover it with foil. Tape the foil underneath to secure it. Use modeling clay, or homemade clay, to form a base around the bottom of the eggshell so it will stand upright, with the opening at the top.

Fill the shell with dirt or potting soil and plant grass seed. Let the pupils draw a man's face on the front of their shell with felt-tip markers. They can glue on construction paper ears, if they like.

Pupils will need to take these home to care for them during the next couple weeks. Have them add one or two spoonfuls of water every day. As the grass grows out of the top of the shells, keep it cut off in a "crew cut."

The children will want to give him a final "haircut" on Father's Day before giving dad their little man.

STAMP HOLDER

Children can make a useful stamp holder for dad from a small matchbox, jewelry box, or package that holds color slides. Decide how to have your pupils finish the boxes according to their age and ability.

Young children could add stars or self-adhesive stickers to the boxes, after the teacher has spray painted them.

Older students can cover the top with macaroni before painting it, or they can spell out "stamps" with alphabet macaroni.

BRICK BOOKENDS

If you have access to a quantity of old bricks, they can be used to make attractive bookends to hold dad's book or record collection.

Each child will need two, smooth, clean bricks that can be given a coat of enamel. Let them dry thoroughly, and then decorate with self-adhesive seals or self-adhesive letters that spell out DAD or his first name.

Cut a piece of felt to fit the bottom of each brick. Glue it in place to protect the table or desk top.

MATCH SCRATCHER

This useful match scratcher will no doubt find a place next to the fireplace, in dad's shop, or with the camping gear.

Each child will need a sheet of colored construction paper, and a sheet *(or one-half sheet)* of sandpaper. Provide a number of simple patterns for "masculine" items, such as a car, truck, tractor, lantern, etc. *(Coloring books are a good source for such patterns.)* Let each child select a pattern and outline it on the back of his sandpaper. Cut it out.

Glue the sandpaper cutout to the center of the sheet of construction paper. Print a favorite Bible verse at the bottom and add a yarn hanger at the top.

MARBLE PAPERWEIGHT

This gift can be made a week ahead *(so it can dry)* or during class on Father's Day *(to dry at home).*

Each child will need his own mold. A waxed milk carton works well. Cut off the carton, leaving only about one inch of the base. Pour into each mold a layer of quick-drying plaster of paris, about three-fourths inch deep.

Before it dries, have the child press glass marbles into the plaster in an even row around the edge of the carton. When the plaster has dried sufficiently, glue a photograph of the child in the center. *(School pictures work well.)*

If this is done a week ahead, let the students remove the carton on Father's Day before taking it home. If done the same day, let children take the paperweight home in the carton. Give them instructions on how to remove it the following day.

STUDENT SILHOUETTES

Dad will treasure this special gift of his child's silhouette.

Begin by discussing how God gave each of us a unique profile—one that other people see, but we seldom see ourselves. Remind them that their fathers could probably recognize them just by the shape of their profile.

You will need a bright lamp, and a sheet of white paper for each child. Seat the child between the lamp and the sheet of paper, which has been taped to the wall. Tape the paper to the wall after the child is seated. That way it can be adjusted so his head and shoulders are in the center of the paper. Have him sit very still while you or a helper carefully outline his profile. Let the child cut it out and mount it on a sheet of black construction paper.

Under the silhouette, glue a strip of paper on which is typed Genesis 1:26a.

Summer

8

PRESCHOOL IDEAS

SEA PICTURES

Preschoolers will enjoy making these sea pictures as part of a summer craft time. Each one will need a sheet of construction paper and two or three fish cut from different colors of construction paper.

Help the children glue the fish in place on the paper. If desired, have them add a few gummed stickers of sea creatures or sea-shells. Put a thin line of glue around the outside edges of the paper. Then cover the whole thing with a sheet of light-blue tissue paper, cut to fit.

SUMMER SUITCASE

You can help prepare your preschoolers for probable vacation trips they will make this summer. They will have fun making a pretend suitcase to take along on their trip.

Fold a 12 x 18 inch sheet of brown construction paper in half. Staple the sides together to form a pocket. Cut an oval hole in the center of the top to make a handle.

Bring to class a supply of magazine or catalog pictures of things they might take on their trip with them. Let them select the items they want to put in their suitcases.

SUMMER CLOTHING

Preschoolers don't fully understand the differences between the seasons. This project will help them to start recognizing some of those differences.

Prepare two large sheets of poster board. Put a sun at the top of one and a snowman at the top of the other.

Bring a number of pictures of children, some dressed in winter clothing and some dressed in summer clothing to class. Cut them from catalogs and magazines. Lay the pictures out on a table, and let the children take turns picking one. Then they decide which poster it belongs on, according to how the children are dressed. Let them glue it to the proper poster. Continue as long as time and space allow.

SUMMER IDEAS

SUMMER SIT-UPONS

If you plan to take your children outside for class during the summer, you may want to make sit-upons to protect their clothing from dampness and dirt.

For each child you will need two eighteen-inch squares of old sheeting, crayons, an eighteen-inch square of plastic cloth, embroidery floss or lightweight yarn, and a large darning needle.

Give each child one piece of sheeting. Have him draw a summer picture on it with crayon. Have him add a favorite Bible verse and his name. Cover the finished picture with a sheet of plain white paper. Then iron with a hot iron to set the crayon picture (right side up). Use a sewing machine and stitch the three pieces together around the edges. Children can then finish their waterproof sit-upon by doing a simple overhand or blanket stitch around the raw edges, using the embroidery floss or yarn and the large needle.

"SANDY" BULLETIN BOARD

Involve your pupils in helping you prepare your summer bulletin board, using the caption: "Jesus Sat Beside the Sea" (Matthew 13:1). Let them make the sandpaper pictures. Start in the center of your board with an appropriate picture of Jesus.

Give each child a sheet of sandpaper and have him draw a beach scene on it with crayons. (Different effects can be achieved by pressing hard or lightly.) The pictures could follow any one of a variety of themes, such as: (1) pictures of sea and sand with no people, (2) Jesus by the sea, (3) the child by the

sea, (4) Jesus and the child beside the sea, etc. Choose a theme and have everyone draw his picture to fit. Display the finished pictures on the bulletin board. Add seashells around the pictures for added interest.

SUMMER DISPLAY PLAQUES

A summer scavenger hunt will produce an interesting variety of leaves, stones, driftwood, shells, and the like. Let your children make display plaques for their special treasures. Coffee grounds make a good background for these nature items. (Dry grounds in the oven.)

Give each child a piece of cardboard to spread with white glue and cover with the dried coffee grounds. When this is dry, they can glue on lightweight items, such as leaves or small shells, to make hanging plaques. Heavier items can be placed on the backgrounds for tabletop displays.

Print the day's memory verse on a small strip of paper and glue it in the bottom, right-hand corner.

SEED PICTURES

Summer is melon time! Take advantage of it and have your pupils save seeds from watermelons, cantaloupes, and other melons. Wash the seeds and lay them out to dry.

Give each child a sheet of construction paper. Have him make a picture by gluing the seeds in place to form a scene. He may want to make a simple outline drawing first and fill in each section with a different kind of seed.

UNDERSEA MURAL

Cover one wall of your classroom, or a large bulletin board, with light-blue or light-green paper. (White may be used if colors are not available.) Draw in simple underwater plants, seashells, and the like to create the setting for an undersea world.

Let the children make different kinds of fish, sea horses, starfish, and other sea creatures from construction paper and glue to the mural. *(Coloring books are an excellent source for these patterns.)*

Use work on the mural as a natural opportunity to discuss God's wonders.

Note: Children may also pick up shells on their vacations to be glued to the mural for a 3-D effect.

COLORFUL SUMMER LEAVES

Take your children out for a short summer walk to collect different kinds of green leaves. If possible, each child should find four different kinds of leaves. Take advantage of the outing to talk about God's beautiful world.

When you return to your room, arrange the leaves on individual sheets of waxed paper, large enough to hold the four leaves. Sprinkle with grated crayon. Cover with another sheet of waxed paper. Put a piece of newspaper on top. Iron until wax and crayon have melted to form a bond. Make a simple frame from brightly-colored construction paper.

BIRDBATHS

Children can help birds survive the hot summer weather by making birdbaths to hang in their backyards.

Each child will need an empty, gallon bleach bottle. Wash the bottles thoroughly and cut a hole in the side of each. *(Plastic is easier to cut if you fill the bottle with hot water to soften. When the plastic is warm, pour out the water and cut.)*

Let the children use permanent, felt-tip markers to print on appropriate, nature-related Bible verses. Then let them decorate the bottles as they wish. A lightweight wire can be tied around the neck of the bottle. Leave the ends long enough to fasten the bath to a tree limb. Keep filled with water.

CLOUD PICTURES

Summer is a wonderful time to go outside and look for animals or other interesting shapes in the clouds. Let pupils make their own "cloud pictures" after they have looked at some of the real thing.

Supply a quantity of white construction paper "clouds" of various sizes and shapes. Give each pupil a sheet of light-blue construction paper. Have him make his own animals or special shapes in his cloud pictures. Glue onto the blue construction paper.

SUMMER EMERGENCY LIST

Because of increased activity during summer months and long dry days, chances of accidents and fire seem to increase. To help remind students to be careful of dangers and more alert to respond, have them make up an "Emergency Response Card" to take home to their families.

Provide a 9 x 6 inch sheet of poster board for each child. Make a list of the emergency phone numbers in your area *(fire, police, ambulance, etc.)*. Have the pupils list clearly the important numbers down the center of their sheet. Then add simple pictures around the edges to decorate it.

When completed, check each one for accuracy and then cover, front and back, with clear, adhesive plastic. Trim the edges even and take home to put near the telephone.

SUMMER EGGS

Sometimes an activity is more fun simply because we do it at an unusual time or in a different place. How about decorating hard-boiled eggs in the summer instead of just at Eastertime?

Plan a class service project to decorate eggs. *(You might try felt-tip markers instead of traditional dyes.)* Deliver them to a class of preschoolers or senior citizens.

SUMMER PAINT-IN

Many teachers avoid painting projects because of the potential mess it might create in the classroom. Take advantage of the opportunity to work outside during the warm, dry summer days. Here are a few ideas to get you started:

Easel Painting: Set up painting easels outside and let children take turns painting pictures.

Sidewalk Painting: If you have a long, smooth sidewalk, roll out a length of butcher paper and let students work together to paint a mural depicting the day's Bible story.

Wall Painting: Tape up a length of butcher paper on a smooth outside wall, instead of on an inside wall.

Rock Painting: Provide large, smooth stones for students to paint. Let them dry in the sun.

MAP HOLDER

This handy map holder can be made at the first of summer for each child to take home as a gift for his family before vacations begin.

Give each child two sheets of poster board, 8½ x 11 inches and 8½ x 7 inches. Staple the small sheet to the front of the larger sheet. Leave the bottom and side edges even and leave a pocket at the top.

Have pupils go through magazines, or a selection of appropriate travel scenes, and cut out pictures to glue to the front of the pocket. Add a meaningful caption, such as: "The Lord Go With Thee." Staple a heavy, yarn handle to the top corners. Then it can be hung from a knob on the car's dashboard and hold the road maps for travel.

CLASSROOM MEMORIES

If your class is going to be promoted at the end of the summer, give them a chance to reminisce about the things they have enjoyed most about the year in your class.

Have each one decide what lesson or activity was the most special or most enjoyable to him. Then draw a picture to illustrate it. He should give the picture a caption.

Display all the pictures on a specially prepared bulletin board under an overall caption, such as: "Special Memories of the Third-Grade Class."

SUMMER SCRAPBOOK

Purchase a scrapbook or make your own with an appropriate picture on the front. Collect a number of magazine pictures showing children involved in a variety of summer-related activities. Older children might enjoy going through summer issues of magazines or catalogs and cutting out their own.

Have the children pick out their favorite pictures to be added to the summer scrapbook. Add captions to each one. Younger children can dictate captions as you write them in.

The summer scrapbook can be left in the classroom to be enjoyed by the children each week, or it can be given to a local children's home or hospital.

Variation: Let an older class make one or more of these summer scrapbooks to be enjoyed by the preschool classes in their own church.

SUMMER RECALL

At the end of the summer, give your pupils an opportunity to share a highlight from their summer. Give each child a 9 x 12 inch sheet of construction paper and a sun cut from bright-yellow construction paper.

Have the children glue the sun in the corner of their paper. Then have them draw a picture depicting their favorite summer memory.

Finished pictures can be used as the child shares an oral report with the class. Later they could be displayed on a special end-of-summer bulletin board.

Independence Day

6

SPECIAL DAYS

Many countries have a special day or week set aside in which they celebrate their independence or liberation. In the United States, July 4 is that important date.

This chapter includes ideas that can be used by almost any country to recognize its patriotic holidays. Some classes may wish to learn about the customs observed in other countries.

Included below is a list of holidays for a number of different countries. They are listed alphabetically.

BAHAMAS—July 10th—Independence Day
BOLIVIA—August 6th—Independence Day
BRAZIL—September 1-7th —Independence Week
CANADA—July 1st—Dominion Day

DENMARK—June 5th—Constitution Day
ENGLAND—November 5th—Guy Fawkes Day
FINLAND—December 6th —Independence Day
FRANCE—July 14th—Bastille Day
INDIA—August 15th—Independence Day
ISRAEL—April 28th—Independence Day
ITALY—June 2nd—Republic Day
JAPAN—February 11th—Empire Day
KOREA—August 15th—Liberation Day
MEXICO—September 15, 16th—Independence Day
NETHERLANDS—May 5th—Liberation Day
PHILIPPINES—June 12th —Independence Day
SWITZERLAND—August 1st—National Day
TURKEY—October 29th—National Day

PATRIOTIC COOKIES

This is an Independence Day craft that your pupils can also eat.

Make or purchase a quantity of plain sugar cookies, enough so each child will have two. Bring to class a bowl of plain butter frosting. Let pupils take turns frosting and decorating their cookies. Provide silver shot and multi-colored sprinkles to use in decorating cookies with flags, stars, liberty bells, firecrackers, or other symbols appropriate to the country's holiday.

FLAG BULLETIN BOARD

This project will provide both a craft and a unique bulletin board display all in one.

You will need a quantity of construction paper strips, 1 x 7 inches, in red, white, and blue (or colors in the country's flag). As pupils arrive, have them start making paper chains (like the ones used on Christmas trees) in each of the different colors. Each chain should be about one foot long for ease in handling. Make several in each color.

As lengths are completed, start tacking them to the bulletin board to form a flag. For a United States flag, be sure you have the proper number of red and white stripes and a blue field for the stars. Add fifty silver, gummed stars. Other flags can be assembled in like manner.

Note: Display the flag, or a picture of it, for pupils to use as a guide. For flags that do not have stripes, or designs adaptable to the rows of chains, make the background or other large areas with chains all in one color. Cut any insignias or odd-shaped pieces from construction paper. Glue them in place over the chains.

PATRIOTIC CRAFT MONTH

Since Independence Day is a reminder of our heritage, it might be a good time to em-phasize the craft skills used by our early settlers or ancestors. Plan to devote craft time each Sunday for a whole month to learning different crafts.

Invite men or women from the congregation to come in and demonstrate different crafts native to the country: embroidery, basket weaving, knitting, crochet, woodcrafts, metal crafts, jewelry making, etc.

Give pupils an opportunity to try their hands at each one. If interest is particularly high in any one area, you might like to plan some craft times other than during class time.

INDEPENDENCE DAY MOBILE

Involve your pupils in making this patriotic mobile to display in the classroom. Use a wire cutter and cut four crossbars from wire hangers (or use four dowels of the same length, about fourteen inches). Cut fishing line or heavy thread into nine pieces of varying lengths. (These will be used to connect the crossbars and suspend the patriotic symbols.)

You will need five different patriotic designs to go on the mobile. Let pupils decide which ones to use, or you may wish to cut them from cardboard before class to save time. Possible designs would include a star, the year, a flag, the country's name or initials, peace sign, firecracker, etc.

Have pupils work together to cover the cardboard designs with glitter. Cover one section at a time with glue and then sprinkle with the appropriate color glitter. Shake excess glitter off onto waxed paper so it can be reused. Move on to the next section and different color of glitter. When one side is completed and dry, turn over and do the back side.

Using the fishing line or string, tie the crossbars together and add the designs.

Note: It helps to tack the top of the mobile to the door frame when you begin to achieve the proper balance of parts. You will need to move the threads along the bars to balance each section as you add each new set of bars or designs. When it is all balanced, put a dab of glue on each knot to keep it in place.

INDEPENDENCE DAY HATS

These patriotic hats can be made by your pupils to wear home in celebration of this special day.

First, cut a hatband for each child, four inches wide and long enough to go around the child's head and overlap. Fold the band in half, lengthwise. Cut three strips of construction paper *(one each of red, white, and blue, or appropriate colors),* five by eighteen inches. Stack the three strips, slip them between the long sides of the band, and staple together in two or three places.

With scissors, cut the three strips into fringe, cutting just to the edge of the hatband. Fit the band around the child's head and staple together.

Note: Fringe can be curled around a pencil so the three colors will show better.

Variation: Other countries can make hats with bands in their country's colors.

SHOE BOX PARADE

Parades are often a part of patriotic celebrations. Let your pupils stage their own special parade by making floats in shoe boxes to commemorate the day.

Divide your class into small groups, or let each child create his own float. Select a theme for your parade that expresses the purpose of the holiday. Let pupils or small groups decide what their float will depict. You may need to lead a discussion on important events connected with Independence Day.

For each float, you will need a shoe box for a base and a variety of materials to use in construction of the float, such as: paper, fab-

ric scraps, spools, egg cartons, ribbon and trims, Styrofoam pieces, small boxes, clay, paper tubes, etc. Encourage your pupils to use their imaginations in their creations.

When the floats are completed, they can be tied together with lengths of string and pulled by a toy truck or tractor. Let someone pull the "parade" and let another pupil or two be "commentators." They should comment on each entry and give background material.

HYMNAL BANDS

Let your class plan a combination craft and service project. Preparations can be made before Independence Day Sunday. Have someone measure around the vertical length of the front cover of your church hymnal, adding one inch for overlap.

Purchase a roll of red, white, and blue wrapping paper *(or appropriate colors for country).* Have pupils cut it in strips about two-inches wide and the measured length. *(See above.)* You will also need some appropriate gummed patriotic seals or large stars to add to the strip.

Invite pupils to meet you at the church on Saturday to put the patriotic bands around all the pew hymnals. Tape the ends together. Add a sticker or star to the front of each strip. These can be easily slipped off after the services.

PATRIOTIC MURAL

Engage your class in preparing a mural on the classroom wall to illustrate a popular patriotic song of your country, such as "America, the Beautiful" for the United States.

Divide the song into phrases. Assign one phrase to each individual or group. They may use crayons, water colors, or felt-tip markers on strips of butcher paper or sheets of poster board to illustrate their phrase.

Discuss the meaning of each phrase before you begin. Sing the song together before and/or after the mural is completed.

WALL FLAG

Select a large, bare wall as the background for a wall-sized flag. Mark off the size of your flag so you can determine the width of the stripes, size of the blue field for the stars, and proportions for other sections of the flag.

Before class, put up the red and white stripes, a blue, construction paper background for the stars, and prepare the background for the United States flag. Put X's on the blue field and mark placement for other designs. Outline fifty stars on white construction paper (after determining size needed to fill field). Older students can outline their own stars if you provide patterns.

In class, divide the stars among the class members. Let them cut out the stars, and then glue them in place on the flag.

Note: Other countries will need to adapt this activity to prepare their own wall flag. Let pupils do as much of it as time allows.

PATRIOTIC POSTER CONTEST

Hold a poster contest to encourage your pupils to think about the meaning of Independence Day. Start with a discussion to encourage each one to make an entry. Select a specific theme, if you wish, and plan to give simple prizes or ribbons for the best posters.

Make arrangements for all posters to be displayed on bulletin boards or easels throughout the church during the appropriate month.

FIRECRACKERS

These "firecrackers" can be made for classroom decorations or filled with candy for a holiday treat.

For each firecracker, you will need one toilet-tissue tube and a piece of construction paper cut to the proper size to cover the outside of the tube.

Have pupils glue the red paper to the outside of their tube. Next, they will trace two circles on pieces of cardboard to cover the open ends. Cut red circles the same size and glue to the cardboard circles. Tape one of the circles to the bottom of the tube.

Decorate each tube with flag stickers, silver stars or other patriotic designs. Punch a hole in the center of the red circle reserved for the top. Push a piece of heavy string or cord through the hole. Tape it underneath to form a "wick." If firecracker is to be used as a decoration, tape the top in place. If it is to be filled with candy, put a piece of tape on one side only for a hinge. It can be filled and then taped shut.

Fall/Promotion 10

LEAF BOYS

Give each child a fall leaf, a sheet of paper, and a black crayon. Have the child glue the leaf to the center of the paper. Then draw on arms and legs to make the leaf into a little "leaf boy." Print the day's memory verse at the bottom of the sheet.

FALL PLACE MATS

Your preschoolers will enjoy making their own fall place mats to use during refreshment times. Bring a variety of fall leaves to class, or encourage your children to bring them.

Give each child a sheet of 9 x 12 inch construction paper for his place mat. Use yellow paper and brown crayons for the rubbings.

Lay a leaf face up on the table. Cover it with the sheet of paper. Show the child how to color over the leaf with the side of the crayon until the design shows up on his paper. The crayon should be rubbed in one direction only. Have him put one rubbing at each end of his place mat.

If you wish to use these place mats all during the fall season, cover them, front and back, with clear, adhesive plastic.

FALL IDEAS

LEAF PICTURES

Older children can be more creative with their leaf rubbings.

Bring a variety of fall leaves to class. Encourage pupils to arrange them in interesting designs or to create animal shapes. Cover the leaves with a sheet of paper and rub over them with the side of a crayon. Rub in one direction.

When finished, have pupils look at the

43

shapes they have created to decide what figures they suggest. Then they may use crayons to fill in the details and complete their pictures.

TREE SCENE

Painted white doilies are the basis for this pretty fall picture. Paint the doilies in fall colors of yellow, orange, and red.

Give each child a sheet of light-blue construction paper on which to glue three doilies in a cluster to represent a group of trees. Over each tree, he will paint a tree trunk. Under each tree he will paint colored leaves on the ground to match the colors of the leaves on the treetops. Add any other details desired to complete the fall scene.

INK-BLOWN TREES

Each pupil will need a sheet of white construction paper and a drinking straw. Mix tempera paint in either black or brown to the consistency of ink. Put a drop in the middle of each sheet of paper. Have the pupil use the straw to blow the paint into the shape of a tree trunk. When the trunk has dried, let him draw and paint or color a few fall leaves on branches.

SPONGE PAINTING

These beautiful fall leaves can be used as classroom decorations or taken home.

Find a pattern, or draw your own, for an eight- to ten-inch oak or maple leaf. Outline the leaf on yellow construction paper for the children to cut out. (You will want to cut them out for younger children.)

Prepare blotting pads of tempera paint in red and orange by putting a cheesecloth pad in the bottom of shallow dishes and soaking with paint. You will need small sponges attached to clip clothespins for each dish of paint.

Cover tables with newspaper (or move outside if weather permits). Give each child a yellow leaf. Have him use the sponge applicator to paint the leaf red. Allow it to dry. Apply orange paint over the red, not covering up the red completely (some of the orange shows through). While painting, discuss the beautiful colors God puts in nature during the fall.

FALL SHADOW BOX

Let your pupils make this shadow box to show off the beauty of a fall bouquet. The base of the shadow box may be made from a paper egg carton or a heavy paper plate.

First, paint the carton or plate with poster paint in a pretty fall color. (Provide a choice of orange, yellow, light green, or brown.) Let dry.

If weather permits, take your pupils outside to collect an assortment of weeds and fall leaves while their boxes are drying. If you can't depend on the weather, bring them from home.

Let pupils select an interesting arrangement of weeds and leaves to staple or tape into place against their prepared shadow box.

POWDERED LEAF PRINTS

Thin white glue with water. Have each pupil paint the back of his leaf with the thinned glue. Carefully press the leaf, glue side down, onto the center of a sheet of yellow construction paper. Remove it quickly from the paper, lifting it straight up. Lay the paper on a cookie sheet (with raised edges) and sprinkle it, while still wet, with a mixture of powdered tempera and sugar. (Let pupils choose from red, orange, or brown. Some may wish to put all three colors on their leaf for a variegated effect.) When the glue is covered, pick up the paper and shake off the excess onto the cookie sheet. The excess can then be returned to the proper container. (If using all three colors, have them shake off the excess of each individually.)

CORNCOB HEADS

When corn on the cob is prevalent in your area, take advantage of it for this fall project.

Each child will need an ear of corn (with the husks on). Begin by pulling the husks up and out from the end to make the "hair." The child may then make a face for his corn man. Cut eyes and a mouth from construction paper and attach with rubber cement. The tip of the corncob, broken off, can be attached with a straight pin for a nose. Let each pupil use his imagination to make his man unique.

Display the "gallery" of corncob heads in your classroom, perhaps hanging them from the ceiling.

PRESERVED LEAVES

Fall leaves can be preserved for craft projects, or just for keeping, by dipping them in a flat dish of liquid wax. Set them out on sheets of waxed paper to dry.

PROMOTION IDEAS

WELCOME FOLDERS

If all your pupils are not being promoted, you will have some remaining to greet the newcomers. They might like to make special welcome cards. (If all students are being promoted, they could still make these before they leave.)

Give each child a 9 x 12 inch sheet of construction paper and a picture of Jesus. Have him fold the sheet of paper in half and glue the picture to the front of the card. Under the picture, print "Welcome to the ___ grade class." He may complete the card by drawing a picture and printing a favorite Bible verse inside, or he might like to write a personal message about what he enjoys most in the class.

Be sure you have enough of these folders so each new pupil will receive one. Some children may need to make more than one.

Variation: Older pupils may wish to make posters to greet newcomers. These posters will prepare newcomers for some of the things they can expect to happen in class during the coming year.

FAMILY TREE

Plan to work on a class "family tree" during the first few weeks after promotion. It's a good way to get acquainted.

If possible, find an actual bare branch, stand it upright in a bucket of sand, and hang a sign from one branch saying, "___ Grade Family Tree."

Provide materials for each pupil to make a small booklet with a construction paper cover and a few pages inside. Cut to size from drawing or typing paper. Ask each pupil to bring a school picture or snapshot from home to glue to the front of his booklet. Inside, he will write a number of facts about himself: name, address, phone number, family members, school attending, hobbies, etc.

Punch a hole in the top corner of each booklet and hang it on the family tree. Each one can look through the books when time permits.

PICTURE NAME TAGS

To help you and your pupils learn more about each other, make these oversized name tags that tell more than a name.

Give each pupil a sheet of construction paper. Have him write his name across the top in big letters. Then have him draw a picture of his whole family engaged in a favorite activity. He can tie a string to the two top corners so he can wear it around his neck.

When the pictures are completed, have the children take turns coming to the front, introducing the members of the family by name, and explaining the activity depicted in the picture.

Note: Take notes as each child shares. Later you can fill in this information on his student record.

CLASS SECURITY BLANKETS

Fall is always a time of new beginnings for children. They go into new classes at school and some in Sunday school also. Teachers need to help make these transitions easy ones, for pupils need to feel secure in their new church environment. "Security blankets" will help them feel at home.

Let your pupils make their own "security blankets" to hang in the classroom for the first few weeks. Hang a length of clothesline along one wall and give each child a square of old sheeting. Ask each one to draw on it a picture of something that makes him happy. Encourage him to add a Bible verse that is comforting. List a few favorites on the chalkboard for him to look up and copy.

Hang the finished "blankets" from the clothesline with clothespins.

PROMOTION CROWNS

To help prepare your pupils for promotion, have each one make a crown to wear to the new class.

Outline the crowns on poster board or gold paper and let the children cut them out.

Now, have them run glue along the outside edges and sprinkle with gold glitter. Shake the excess off onto a sheet of newspaper so it can be reclaimed. Staple each crown to fit the child's head.

CLASS YEARBOOK

This yearlong project needs to be started the first Sunday after promotion and continued through the year. It can be used with any age group, but the older the students the greater their involvement. With younger children, you will want to select a new editor every two weeks or every month.

On the first Sunday, take a photograph of the class *(or of individual pupils, if you prefer)*. Have the pupils prepare a scrapbook. This can be a purchased book, to which they add appropriate decorations and the class name, or it can be made with a poster board cover, pages cut to fit, and held together with loose-leaf rings.

The class photo(s) will go on the first page. Each week a copy of the week's handwork, comments about anything special that happened, or a photo of a class event can be added by that week's editor.

At the end of the Sunday-school year, the book can be shared with parents and/or reviewed by the class.

OUR CLASS

Working together is one of the best ways to mold a group of children into a class. This activity will help move you toward that goal.

Decide on a symbol to represent your class. It could be a cross, the numeral for the class grade, or something related to the lessons you will be studying. Cut the symbol from a large sheet of poster board. Make it as large as possible.

On the first Sunday after promotion—or shortly thereafter—present the symbol project to your new class. Before class, cut the symbol into puzzle pieces, one for each member plus a few extras. *(Be sure to number the pieces to make it easier to reassemble later.)*

Give each child a piece of the puzzle and ask him to decorate it to reveal something about himself. This could include a picture, his address, his phone number, his birthdate, his hobbies, etc.

When the pieces have been decorated, work together to reassemble them on a prepared bulletin board. Add the extra pieces to the puzzle to complete the shape.

Complete the bulletin board by adding a picture of each child, if possible. Tack the picture near his piece and join the two with a piece of ribbon or yarn.

Thanksgiving 11

THANKSGIVING SCRIPTURES

Following is a list of Scriptures on praise and thanksgiving. You will find them useful when preparing crafts and handwork for the Thanksgiving season.

Leviticus 23:33-44 (feast of booths)

1 Chronicles 16:8	Psalm 106:1
1 Chronicles 16:34	Psalm 140:13
1 Chronicles 23:30	Psalm 147:7
1 Chronicles 29:13	Daniel 2:23a
Psalm 26:7	Matthew 15:36
Psalm 30:4	1 Corinthians 15:57
Psalm 30:12	2 Corinthians 2:14
Psalm 34:1	2 Corinthians 9:11
Psalm 67:3	2 Corinthians 9:15
Psalm 69:30	Ephesians 5:20
Psalm 75:1	Philippians 4:6
Psalm 79:13	Colossians 1:12
Psalm 92:1	Colossians 3:17
Psalm 95:2	Colossians 4:2
Psalm 100:4	1 Thessalonians 5:18
Psalm 105:1	1 Timothy 4:4

PRESCHOOL IDEAS

THANKSGIVING DINNER

Prepare your children ahead of time for their Thanksgiving dinner by helping them create a plate full of "pretend" dinner.

Before class, prepare a large paper plate for each child. Print around the border of the plate "Thank You, God, for this food." Have ready a quantity of magazine pictures of food, cut into small, individual portions.

After a discussion of the traditional Thanksgiving dinner, let the children select the portions of food they want to include in their dinner. Let them glue these to the center of their plates.

THANKFUL MURAL

Put up a length of butcher paper on your classroom wall. Use it to make a mural to remind your preschoolers of the many things they are thankful for.

Across the top of the paper print "God Made Everything." Across the bottom print "Thank You, God." Have ready a collection of magazine pictures of things for which children might thank God.

Let the children select pictures and glue them in place on the mural. When the mural is finished, or as you work, discuss with the children their selection of pictures.

HAND TURKEY

Teach your children how to make a simple turkey, using their hand as a pattern. Have each child put his hand in the middle of a sheet of paper, with his thumb outstretched and fingers spread apart. Trace around it with a brown crayon. Let him use crayon to close in the bottom of the body and add legs and an eye. He may color the tail feathers in bright colors.

THANKS BOOKLET

Following a discussion of the many things for which we need to thank God, let your pupils prepare these booklets to take home as a reminder.

Each child will need two sheets of typing paper folded in half and stapled together at the fold. Bring to class a number of pictures that show the things your small children are thankful for: home, family, mother, father, flowers, birds, sun, moon, stars, pets, church, Jesus, friends, etc.

At the top of the front page print "Thank You, God." Let each child pick out his own pictures and glue them to the pages of his book.

SEED POSTERS

Talk to your children about how God planned for food to grow from seeds. Show a number of seed packets with the picture of the food on the outside. Then let them see the seeds from which that food will grow.

Give each child a sheet of construction paper on which you have printed "Thank You, God, for food." Let the child spread some glue around on his paper. Then let him sprinkle it with different seeds from the packets. Excess seeds can be shaken off onto a cookie sheet and reused.

THANKFUL FOOTPRINTS

This activity will help your preschoolers to be thankful for their feet and being able to walk.

Have each child remove his shoes so you can outline his feet on a piece of construction paper. Under the feet print "Thank You, God, for walking feet."

Let the child color and decorate his feet as he wishes.

THANKSGIVING CRAFTS

PAPER PLATE TURKEY

This simple turkey can be made by pupils and then taken home to be used as a centerpiece for the family's Thanksgiving dinner.

Each child will need a twelve-inch paper plate folded in half (inward) and stapled at the top to hold. Paint it with brown poster paint and let dry. Provide a pattern for a turkey head of brown poster board. After the head is made, slip the neck between the front edges of the plate and staple in place.

Give each child a pattern for tail feathers. Let him trace the pattern and cut several feathers from different colors of construction paper. Before slipping these feathers into the body and stapling in place, the child should write something he is thankful for on each feather. He could write something on each side of each feather, since they will be seen from both sides of the table.

The finished bird will stand upright in a ball of clay.

TABLE PRAYERS

Early in November, check with a restaurant near your church that will be serving dinner on Thanksgiving Day. Ask if your pupils can place "prayer reminders" on their tables for the holiday. Find out the number of tables.

Divide the number of "reminders" needed between your pupils, so you will have enough for each table. Give each pupil the needed number of five-inch squares of orange construction paper or poster board. Have them fold the squares in half. Provide praying-hands stickers to be attached to the left-hand side of one half. Next to the sticker put a Thanksgiving Scripture that has been typed out and duplicated. *(You might be able to find appropriate Scriptures on gummed stickers that you could use.)*

Stamp the back half of each "reminder" with your church's name and address, or attach a church business card. *(Business cards will be more durable if you cover the front of each one with clear, self-adhesive plastic.)*

SONG OF THANKS

Prepare your bulletin board or a classroom wall for this month-long Thanksgiving project. Put up a large music staff with a treble clef on the left-hand side. At the top add the caption "Sing a Song of Thanks."

Each Sunday give every pupil present a music note. Let him write on it something for which he is thankful. Let him decorate it as he wishes. Then he may add it to the staff.

Variation: Select a familiar Thanksgiving song and mark the location for each note on the staff. As children add their notes to the staff each week, they will be writing the music for the song.

SEED TURKEY

Older pupils will love the challenge of making a seed turkey plaque they can display at home during the Thanksgiving holiday.

For each pupil you will need a twelve-inch-square sheet of quarter-inch plywood or cardboard. Have the pupils paint the cardboard with orange tempera or sand and stain the plywood.

Give each one an outline of a turkey cut from construction paper or poster board. *(A front view with head, body, and tail clearly outlined works best.)* Glue the outline to the plywood or cardboard. Black yarn can be glued around the outline for added emphasis, if desired.

Provide several containers of different kinds of seeds, kernels of dried or Indian corn, etc. Use white glue and cover only one section at a time. Cover the section liberally with glue and add one kind of seed.

THANKSGIVING "NEWS"

For this craft project, you will need a supply of want-ad sections and Sunday comics from your newspaper. Also supply a variety of patterns for Thanksgiving-related silhouettes, such as: pilgrim man and woman, Indian man and woman, turkey, tree, cornstock, etc. Or, instead, you may wish to put the emphasis on things the pupils would be thankful for, such as: church, Bible, house, birds, flowers, etc.

A pupil will begin by deciding what his picture will depict and selecting a piece of brightly colored construction paper for a background. He will then choose the proper patterns and cut silhouettes from the want-ad sections. These will be glued in place to make the Thanksgiving scene. He may need to cut some figures freehand to complete his picture.

Display the finished pictures on a bulletin board under the caption "Happy Thanksgiving," cut from the Sunday comic sections.

THANKSGIVING PLACE MATS

These place mats can be made by your pupils and used for refreshment times during the month of November.

Give each child a sheet of light-colored construction paper. Have him draw a border of foods he likes to eat all around the edge. Provide a different, simple table grace, typed out, for each child. He may choose one grace and glue it to the center of his place-mat. Each week, let one or more children read their grace before refreshments.

THANKFUL TURKEY

A giant turkey bulletin board or classroom wall will be the center of attention. Begin by hanging up an oversized turkey body and head *(no tail).* This could be cut from butcher paper and appropriately painted.

Tell your pupils that it will be their responsibility to provide the tail for the turkey. Give them pieces of construction paper in yellow, orange, and brown. Have them outline their hands, fingers spread, on several pieces of the paper. For each handprint, they must find a Bible verse that contains a form of the word "thank" and write it on. Show them how to use a concordance, and then set out a few for their use.

They each may prepare as many Scripture-verse hands as they like. Thumbtack *(or tape)* the hands in place on the turkey, over-lapping them to make a full tail *(fingers pointing away from the turkey).*

PAPER BAG INDIAN SKINS

Thanksgiving is a good time to emphasize the place of Indians in our heritage. Provide some books from the library that show Indian signs and what they mean. After you have shared the books with the children, let them make their own authentic looking animal "hides." Each child will need a large grocery bag, opened up at the seams so it will lay

flat. It should then be torn to resemble the shape of a bearskin rug. Wad up the paper several times and then smooth it out to soften.

Have each pupil select the designs that he wants to use and add them to his hide in crayon or poster paint. They might like to try and tell the Thanksgiving story using their Indian symbols.

DOORKNOB HANGERS

This craft project will be in preparation for a special Thanksgiving service project.

Before class, cut several patterns for a doorknob hanger. It should be about eight inches long and two and a half inches wide, with a hook at the top for hanging.

Have pupils use patterns to cut out hangers from brightly-colored construction paper or poster board. Each pupil will want to make at least six more if time permits. Pupils can print on the message, or you may type it out and duplicate it so they can just glue it to the hanger. The message could be "Thank You, God, for everyone. Thank You, God, for neighbors." Decorate the hangers with Thanksgiving stickers.

Encourage pupils to sign their names before they distribute them in their neighborhoods.

Variation: The church's name could be stamped at the bottom and distributed to the homes around the church.

STRETCH TURKEY

These decorative turkeys will make nice door hangings for pupils' front doors during November.

Have each pupil bring a wire hanger and a pair of clean, discarded panty hose. Bend the hanger into an oval shape to form the body of the turkey. Bend the hook on the hanger into shape to make a head. Insert the hanger into a leg of the panty hose, avoiding portions with runs. Tie with string around the neck. If it must be tied on the other side, also, do it where the tail feathers will hide it. Then cut off any excess fabric.

Provide patterns so students can cut heads and wings from brown construction paper. Cut tail feathers from multicolored construction paper. A simple wing can be made from a half circle with slashes around the curved edge to represent feathers. Glue or staple the parts in place. Add details with felt-tip markers.

THANK-YOU CANS

Have each child bring to class a coffee or shortening can with a plastic lid. You will also need a supply of magazine pictures that represent things for which your children are thankful.

Using white glue, glue the pictures to the can like a collage. Dry thoroughly and spray with clear shellac. Dry and give it a second coat if needed.

Encourage children to take their cans home to use as a storage can and as a prayer reminder of the things for which they are thankful. They might like to put their prayer requests in the can also. Glue a special Thanksgiving Scripture to the lid, if desired.

INDIAN "WAMPUM"

Explain to the children that during the time of the Pilgrims "wampum" was used for money. "Wampum" was made by the Indians from shells that were polished, drilled with a hole in the center, and strung together.

Let the children make their own "wampum" by stringing cereal or candy with a hole in the middle on a cord. Tie the ends together so the children can wear them around their necks.

Variation: Have pupils bring two or three small items from home to "sell" to their classmates. Let them set a price for each item *(in pieces of wampum)* and start trading with each other.

Christmas

12

TISSUE WREATH

Your preschoolers will have fun making this easy, but attractive, wreath to take home and hang on their bedroom door.

Before class, cut green tissue paper into twelve-inch squares, and cut red yarn into twelve-inch lengths. Each child will need several squares of tissue, one piece of yarn, and a twelve-inch paper plate with the center cut out. *(Save the center circle.)*

Give each child several pieces of tissue and a plate with his name written on the back. Use the paper-plate center to hold a spot of glue for each child. Have him wad each square of tissue into a ball, dip one side in the glue, and stick it on his plate. Repeat until ring is covered. Punch two holes at the top of each plate. Then thread a loop of red yarn through as a hanger.

BED FOR BABY JESUS

Each child will need a small, white envelope *(the size invitations usually come in).* Seal each envelope. Then carefully cut a slit across the front panel only, one to one-and-a-half inches from one end.

Have each child color the "bed" the way he wants to prepare it for baby Jesus. Each "baby" will be made from a flat ice-cream spoon *(or cut in the same shape from pink poster board).* Let each child draw a face on his spoon. He can put the baby to bed by slipping it into the slit in the envelope.

CHRISTMAS BOOKMARKS

Preschoolers can make these simple holiday bookmarks as gifts for their parents or others.

For each bookmark you will need a six-inch length of red or green fabric ribbon, one and one-half inches wide. Cut the ends on a slant or with pinking shears.

Provide a variety of self-adhesive Christmas stickers. Let the children add three or four of them to the right side of each bookmark.

CHRISTMAS ORNAMENTS

Provide a variety of three- to four-inch Christmas shapes cut from red and green construction paper, such as: bells, trees, birds, stars, angels, etc.

Let pupils select one or two shapes and lay them on a sheet of waxed paper. Give them a small bottle of white glue to make a scribble design on the front of each shape. *(Be sure bottles are opened only enough to let out a thin line of glue.)*

Next, they will sprinkle the shapes with silver glitter, being careful to cover all lines of the glue. Shake excess off onto the waxed paper. Punch a hole at the top of each ornament and add a yarn hanger.

CHRISTMAS CARDS

BURLAP CHRISTMAS CARD

Each child will need:
    1 4 x 4½ inch piece of cardboard
    1 piece natural-color burlap, 4 x 5 inches
    1½ inch length of yellow chenille wire
    1 2 x 3 inch piece of red plastic yardage
    1 8 inch piece of red string
    1 1 x 2 inch piece of white card stock
    1 sprig of evergreen

Instructions:
1. Use white glue to glue the piece of burlap to the cardboard, centering it with a one-fourth inch overlap at each end.
2. Fringe the overlap by pulling out the crossways threads.
3. Fold the piece of red plastic to form a three by one inch tube. Glue it, centered vertically, on the front of the card, seam hidden to form a candle.

4. Trim one end of the chenille wire to a point. Then bend it into an elongated "S" shape. Glue in place inside the top of the red candle to represent a flame.
5. Punch a hole in one corner of the white card. Fold the piece of red string in half. Thread the fold of the string through the hole in the card. Put loose ends of the string through the loop to secure string on the card.
6. Tape loose ends of string to bottom of candle.
7. Cover the ends of the string and the bottom of the candle with a sprig of evergreen, gluing it in place.
8. A Christmas greeting can be written on one side of the card and the giver's name on the back of it.

YARN CHRISTMAS CARD

Pupils can make this unusual Christmas card for their parents with a 3-D decoration on the front.

Give each child half of a 9 x 12 inch sheet of red construction paper to fold in half like a card. Draw a simple Christmas tree on the front. Run a line of glue across the bottom of the tree and add pieces of green yarn *(cut into one-inch lengths)* vertically to make the first row of needles. About three-fourths inch up, run another line of glue. Add more yarn in a row that slightly overlaps the first row. Continue moving up and adding rows until the entire tree is covered.

Glue multicolored sequins to the yarn to make ornaments. Put a gold gummed star on the top. Color in a black or brown trunk at the bottom.

Let dry and then have pupils write in an appropriate holiday greeting for their parents.

DO-IT-YOURSELF CARDS

Christmas cards are much more personal when the children use their creativity to make their own.

Since you will want an envelope to hold each of these cards, cut red, white, or green construction paper to fit the available envelopes *(either flat or folded).*

Give pupils a supply of used Christmas cards. From these they can cut scenes or objects to add to their own cards. Glue in place. Have them print on a Christmas Scripture reference or a short verse. Finish decorating the cards with gummed stars, holiday stickers, cotton clouds, straw, or however they wish.

They may want to make several cards if time permits.

TREE ORNAMENTS

TASSEL ORNAMENTS

Make unique Christmas tree ornaments from the white, foam packing material that is shaped like peanut shells.

For each ornament, make a small tassel from red or green yarn, leaving a length of yarn attached. This tassel will be the bottom of the ornament. Put a needle on the end of the yarn and thread on the foam pieces, alternating with pieces of construction paper cut into small Christmas shapes, such as stars or bells. Vary the length of the ornaments or make them all the same length.

The construction paper may be red, green, multicolored, or selected to fit your holiday color scheme. Finish the ornaments by tying a loop at the top of the yarn for hanging on the tree.

Variation: The tassel can be replaced with a small tag that has a Christmas verse from the Bible typed on it.

CHRISTMAS CARD ORNAMENTS

Make cardboard patterns of three- or four-inch circles *(or simple Christmas shapes).*

Have pupils use the patterns to cut circles from suitable portions of two different, old Christmas cards for each ornament. Glue the circles, back to back, with a three-inch length of florist's wire sandwiched between them. *(Be sure enough of the wire extends from the top of the circles to bend into a hook for hanging.)*

The edges of the ornaments can then be finished as desired. Glue rickrack or ribbon around each edge, decorate edges with glue and glitter, or add sequins, beads, or other trims. Put a small ribbon bow at the top in a coordinated color.

DOUGH-ART ORNAMENTS

Make dough, using one part salt, one part water, and two parts flour. Combine flour and salt, add water gradually, and knead dough until firm—about eight to ten minutes.

To make ornaments, roll dough about one-fourth inch thick and cut with Christmas cookie cutters. *(Simple, metal cutters work best.)* Use a nail to make a hole in the top of the ornament for hanging.

Use a fork to make designs in the soft dough. Add 3-D additions by shaping small pieces of dough. Moisten the back of them before putting in place.

Put ornaments on a cookie sheet and bake at 325° until hard—about 30 minutes. Apply varnish to the cooled ornaments to preserve them. They can be decorated more with glue and glitter or poster paint. Thread a length of yarn through the hole. Tie into a loop for hanging on the tree.

GINGERBREAD MEN

For a variation of the dough-art ornaments, let your pupils make these enchanting gingerbread men.

Make the dough as before, but cut out a gingerbread man for each child, plus extras for visitors and catastrophes. Punch a hole in the top of each with a nail. *(If you want to spend two sessions on these, and you have the facilities, pupils can cut out their own men the first week.)* Bake at 325° for about thirty minutes.

In class, give each child a gingerbread man. Have him cut the head from one of his school pictures and glue it onto the head of his man. Cut black, construction paper circles with a hole punch. Glue three or four into place for buttons. Add additional decorations with colored pens and spray with shellac. When dry, tie a piece of red yarn through the hole and make a loop. Parents will love this personalized ornament to hang on their tree.

PRETZEL SNOWFLAKES

Pretzels make interesting window or tree decorations that birds will enjoy eating after Christmas. Use large pretzels for window decorations, and small ones for tree ornaments.

Give each child six twisted pretzels. Have him gather them into a circle *(five around the outside and one in the center)* on a sheet of waxed paper. Put generous dabs of glue on all points of contact, where one pretzel touches another. Original creations can be made by gluing on pieces of dry cereal or macaroni. Let dry.

The next Sunday remove the waxed paper carefully. Tie a red ribbon through one of the pretzel loops to hang. After Christmas, hang them on an outside tree branch for birds to eat.

YARN-PAINTING ORNAMENTS

Let your children experiment with yarn ornaments made by a process similar to yarn painting in Mexico.

Cut simple cardboard shapes in Christmas designs: stars, angels, bells, trees, wreaths, birds, etc. Using a glue stick for adhesive, outline the entire design in one color of yarn, both outside and inside lines. Using one or more additional colors of yarn, and working from the outside edges, fill in each area with a continuous strand of yarn swirled around to fill outlined areas completely.

When one side is finished and dry, turn the figure over and repeat on the second side *(or cover the back with felt)*. Use a needle to add a thread loop for hanging on the tree.

CHRISTMAS CRAFTS

CHRISTMAS NAPKIN RINGS

Your pupils will enjoy making Christmas napkin rings as gifts for family members and friends for their holiday dinner.

Ahead of time collect or ask children to bring cardboard tubes *(from paper towels)* to provide a two-inch length of tube for each napkin ring. You will also need old Christmas cards, white glue, and red and green rug yarn or rickrack.

Cut a pretty section of the Christmas cards into two-inch-wide strips, long enough to go around tubes and overlap about one-half inch. Glue a card strip around each two-inch piece of tubing. Children may hold strips in place until they dry, or hold them with paper clips. When dry, glue a row of yarn or rickrack around both cut edges of each ring.

A small name tag can be added to each ring, if desired.

CHRISTMAS THEME PLAQUES

Give a red or green paper plate to each child. Have each one decide on a holiday theme, and choose a number of old Christmas cards that express that theme, such as: angels, snowmen, nativity scene, Mary and Jesus, shepherds, Wise-men, etc. *(Encourage each one to select a different theme as much as possible.)*

Cut the pictures from the cards. Arrange them collage style on the plate and glue in place. Glue a ribbon hanger to the back of the plate.

CHRISTMAS TREES

These candy-filled trees can be made as gifts for parents or friends, or as a special project for a children's hospital, orphanage, mission station, etc.

Each child will need a wedge-shaped plastic pie container, an empty thread spool, and a piece of green felt cut to fit the lid of the container. He will also need a piece of felt cut to make a band around the center portion of the thread spool. Glue the felt pieces in place.

Next, let him pick any trims he wishes to use to decorate his "tree." Glue them into place on the green felt. Give him a choice of trims, such as: sequins, gold braid, glitter, rickrack, pearls, beads, and other trims. When the tree is decorated, glue the trunk in the proper place on the end of the container. Let it dry.

Later, have him fill his "tree" with nuts or candy. Arrange to have them delivered to their prearranged destination.

CHRISTMAS TREE VERSE PANELS

Give each child a sheet of construction paper. Tell him to imagine that he is looking at just one section of a Christmas tree. Then have him draw several branches (detailing the needles) on the paper with crayon.

Next, cut about four three-inch ornaments from colored construction paper. Glue to the branches in appropriate places. Supply a number of memory verses, typed on small slips of paper, and let each child select a verse to glue to the center of each ornament. Decorate the ornaments.

CHRISTMAS WINDOWS

Cut a piece of muslin or an old sheet (without holes) the size of your bulletin board, plus enough to turn under the raw edges all the way around. Iron it, pressing under the edges, and tack it to the bulletin board.

Divide the fabric into equal squares, enough for each pupil plus visitors. Use a permanent felt marker or fabric crayon. (Fill any extra squares with Christmas greetings or the class name and date.) Assign a square to each pupil. Have him use fabric crayons to draw a Christmas scene on it and sign his name. Let two or three work at a time, as space permits. The others can be planning their picture on a sheet of scratch paper.

Add "Merry Christmas 19__" in cutout letters above or to the side of the board.

THREAD SPOOL CRÈCHE

This classroom crèche will take on special meaning for your pupils if they create the figures themselves. And you can save it to use for many years.

A week before you start, ask each pupil to bring in new spools of thread (specify size and type of spool) in the following colors to make these figures (divide number equally between pupils): Mary—two light blue and one light pink, Joseph—two medium brown and one light pink, baby Jesus—one white and one light pink, shepherd—two avocado green and one light pink, sheep—two whites, Wise-men—two purple and one light pink, two red and one light pink, two gold and one light pink.

Assign one or more pupils to work on each figure. To make the people, stack three spools together (two for the baby) with the pink one on top for the head. Let pupils use felt and their imaginations to complete each figure. Mary, Joseph, and the shepherd should have headdresses made from felt—in colors to match their thread. Make the shepherd a staff from a bent chenille wire. Use a chenille wire to make an arm so he can hold it out in front of him (other figures won't need arms).

Make crowns for the Wise-men from gold braid and trims. The sheep are made from one spool of thread with a cotton ball for a head, a little piece of cotton for a tail and nose, and bent chenille wires for legs. Baby

Jesus will need felt hair, and all the other figures may have felt features glued in place, including felt beards for the men. A square of tan felt, fringed around the edges, will represent hay for the baby to lie on.

Cover a box lid with brown paper for the stable. Surround it with evergreens and set up the crèche.

Note: If purchasing thread is a problem, empty spools may be covered with bands of felt in the designated colors.

EASY-TIE WREATH

This unusual wreath will be an interesting project for your pupils. Before class, cut a large quantity of 2 x 8 inch strips from ribbon, fabric, crepe paper, and Christmas wrap. For a two-session project, provide patterns and let students cut the strips.

Give each one a hanger and have him bend it into a circle, leaving the hook at the top. Alternating strips of different materials, carefully tie the strips to the hanger, making one loose knot in the center of each strip. Keep pushing the strips close together. Keep adding to it until the wreath looks very full. When completed, add a large red, crepe-paper bow to the hook at the top. Send it home to be hung in a window or on a door.

HOLIDAY PAPER CHAIN

Class preparation of Christmas tree decorations can fill a double purpose. As the pupils are making paper chains for your tree, give each one several 1 x 4 inch strips of colored construction paper. Have him write on each one the name of a relative or friend, or a special request, that he wants the class to remember during prayer time *(one name or one request to a strip).* Assemble the chain by looping the strips together and gluing. Hang the finished chain on your classroom tree.

Each week preceding Christmas, when it is time for prayer, have each child go to the tree and select one or two "links." *(Ask for further explanation as needed.)* If pupils do not wish to discard their "prayer chain" when the tree is taken down, you might want to hang it on the wall and continue to use it for a few weeks.

GLITTER PLAQUES

Easy Christmas plaques can be made from plastic lids found on coffee cans, shortening cans, whipped topping containers, and the like. Select ones that have a raised edge around the outside. You will need one for each pupil.

Let each child select a picture from the front of an old Christmas card. Have him cut it to fit inside the raised edge of the lid. Glue it in place. Carefully spread glue around the raised "frame" and sprinkle it with glitter. Shake off the excess glitter onto a sheet of waxed paper so it can be reused. Add a yarn or ribbon hanger at the top.

GIFT PIN FOR MOTHER

To make a special gift pin for mother, cut two small Christmas trees or holly leaves from green felt *(provide patterns).* Glue them together. Sew a small safety pin to the back. Decorate by gluing multicolored sequins to the tree for ornaments, or cover the holly leaf with green sequins, putting three red ones near the stem for berries.

These would also make nice gifts for women patients in a nursing home. They could wear them on a bed jacket or robe during the holidays.

Other Special Times

13

This chapter includes ideas for crafts and projects that can be carried out for many special times during the year. On the following pages you will find ideas for May Day, Family Week, Memorial/Veterans' Day, Children's Sunday, Columbus Day, and Children's Book Week.

MAY DAY

FLOWER CARDS

These cards can be prepared by children to take home as gifts for parents. Or several can be made in class and taken home to deliver to their neighbors on May 1. *(If they are to be saved for May Day, students can make the cards in class and then add fresh flowers from their own yards later.)*

For each card you will need a 4 x 6 inch piece of poster board in a pretty pastel color. With a hole punch, punch two holes, about one inch apart, along one side of the card.

Have the child write "God Loves You—I Love You" on the front of the card. Thread the stem of a flower through the two holes, trimming off the end if it is too long.

DOILY BASKET

For each simple basket for mother, or to leave on a friend's door, the children will need doilies and a piece of ribbon.

For each basket, give pupils two or three white paper doilies that have not been separated. Cut a piece of sturdy ribbon about six-inches long. Fold the doilies and the ribbon in half without creasing either one. Slip the cut edges of the ribbon into the top, middle of the basket and staple in place.

Provide a variety of small, cut flowers to be slipped into each side of the basket.

SPOOL HOLDERS

Each child will need an empty thread spool and a variety of small, artificial flowers. Decorate the spool first by covering it with a strip of colored construction paper or felt *(glued in place)*, or decorate with crayons or felt-tip markers. Put a small ball of clay in the bottom of the hole.

A green chenille wire, with construction paper leaves attached, can be put in the hole along with two or three small flowers to make a mini bouquet. If the stems are long enough to stick into the clay, they will stay in place better.

MAY PLAQUES

Unlike fresh-flower bouquets, these reminders will last indefinitely.

Around the first of April, instruct pupils to pick several fresh, spring flowers. At home press them between waxed paper in a big book. They will need to stack several other large books on top to help with the pressing.

Two Sundays before May Day, have them bring their pressed flowers to class *(inside the book)*. Each child will need a plastic lid with a raised edge in which to arrange his pressed flowers. Carefully pour liquid plastic over the flowers. When set, remove the plaque from the lid and it will be ready to give as gift.

MAY PICTURE

To make these spring pictures, each pupil will need a sheet of pastel-colored construction paper (9 x 12 inches), flower blossoms cut from construction paper, cotton balls, a green crayon, and perfume.

Give each child a sheet of paper and from one to three paper blossoms. Have him arrange the blossoms at the top of the sheet and glue in place. Use the green crayon to draw on stems and leaves. Then glue a cotton ball to the center of each blossom. Add a dash of perfume to each cotton center.

Provide each child with an appropriate Scripture or spring poem that has been typed on a slip of paper. He can glue it on his picture next to the bouquet.

FAMILY WEEK
(Week Preceding Mother's Day)

FAMILY PORTRAITS

Give each child a sheet of drawing paper and have him draw pictures of the members of his family—and any members of his "extended family" *(friends, neighbors, or relatives)* who are important to him.

When the pictures are completed, let each child show his picture and tell the class about the people in his family portrait.

MY HOME AND FAMILY

Before the class meets, contact the parents of your pupils and ask them to send a family snapshot to class.

Give each child a 12 x 18 inch sheet of construction paper or poster board to be used as a background. Let him choose a piece of 9 x 12 inch construction paper the same color as his house. Have him draw a simple outline of his house on the paper, making it as large as possible. Then have him cut it out. Use picture corners to mount the family photograph in the center of the house cutout. Then have him print his last name over the picture and his address under it. Glue this house to the left-hand side of the background sheet.

Provide a simple outline pattern in the proper size for a telephone to fit next to the house. Have each child cut out his phone, glue it to his poster, and write his telephone number across the front of it. Add the caption, "My Home and Family" across the top of the poster.

FAMILY TOTEM POLES

Let your children make special gifts for the members of their families in remembrance of Family Week. Alert the pupils several weeks ahead to save cardboard cones from paper towels and bring them to class *(or you provide them)*. Each child will need one for every member of his immediate family *(those living at home)*.

Before beginning, have each pupil list his family members by name. Then next to each one on his list write as many of that person's favorite things and interests as he can remember.

When he has made his list, let him make a "totem pole" for each family member. At the top he will put a picture of the person's face. Under that he will put symbols to represent different interests. *(He can draw these on pieces of construction paper, cut them out, and glue in place on the pole.)* Remind him not to forget appropriate religious symbols, such as: cross, Bible, and praying hands.

Variation: If this is too time-consuming, have pupils make one totem pole for the whole family, putting on a face and one symbol for each person.

MY HOUSE

Preschoolers will enjoy this simple project during Family Week.

Give each child a 9 x 12 inch sheet of construction paper you have folded across the middle. *(You may want to let them pick a piece of paper in the same color as their house.)* Tuck in the upper corners on the fold to form the shape of a roof. The house will then be able to stand up.

Have each child draw windows and a door on the front of his house. Encourage him to draw a picture of his family on the inside.

MEMORIAL/VETERANS' DAYS

AIRPLANES

For each plane you will need a cellophane-wrapped candy stick for the body, a wrapped stick of gum for the wings, two white, mint Lifesavers for wheels, two gummed stars, and a rubber band.

To assemble, hold the piece of gum across one end of the candy stick *(to form wings)*. Thread the two Lifesavers onto the rubber band and push them to the center. Loop the two ends of the rubber band over each side of the stick of gum to hold it in place. Position one "wheel" on each side of the candy stick. Cut a slip of paper the same width as the stick of gum and one-half inch shorter. On the slip write an appropriate Bible verse. Center the slip on the wings of the plane. Use a gummed star at each end to hold it in place.

COMMEMORATIVE BULLETIN BOARDS

From the church office, get a list of church members or family members of church people who are serving in the armed forces. Contact these families and borrow a picture of each service man or woman *(in uniform if possible)*.

Have your pupils design a bulletin board using a patriotic theme with flags, bunting, or the like. Display each person's picture and name. This bulletin board should emphasize the need to pray for these service people.

Variation: On a similar bulletin board, you could highlight a list of veterans within the church body. Or you could prepare a memorial board recognizing church family members who have been killed in military service.

CHILDREN'S SUNDAY

CHILDREN'S SUNDAY BANNERS

Involve older children in making child-related banners to display around the church on Children's Sunday *(and to be displayed later in the classrooms)*.

Have each class choose an appropriate

Bible passage or quotation concerning children. *(See list below.)* Use it on a felt banner.

Cut felt yardage to the desired size for each banner. Machine or hand stitch a casing across the top into which a piece of doweling can be inserted. Nail or tie a piece of cord to each end of the dowel to form a hanger. Fringe the lower edge of the felt by cutting slashes with scissors across the full width.

Provide patterns for small block letters so pupils can cut them from felt or other fabric in contrasting colors. Glue in lace to spell out the selected verse, motto, quotation, etc. Add appropriate decorations as desired.

Scriptures

Psalm 8:2a	Matthew 18:3
Psalm 34:11	Matthew 18:5
Psalm 127:3	Mark 9:36, 37
Proverbs 20:11	Mark 10:14
Proverbs 22:6	Mark 10:15
Proverbs 22:15	Luke 9:48
Proverbs 29:15	1 Corinthians 13:11
Ecclesiastes 11:10	Ephesians 6:1
Isaiah 11:6	Ephesians 6:2

CHILDREN'S SUNDAY MURAL

Younger children can prepare a mural for Children's Sunday that can be displayed on a hallway wall in the church for all to enjoy.

Hang a length of butcher paper on the wall. Provide a number of magazine pictures that show children involved in a variety of activities. Also have Scripture verses *(above list)*, poems, quotations, etc. concerning children available. Let the pupils glue all of these to the mural in a collage.

CHILDREN'S SUNDAY POSTER CONTEST

Hold a poster contest prior to Children's Sunday. Ask the children to submit posters that carry out a particular theme, such as: "Kids Are People, Too" or "I Am a Child of

God." Encourage them to be as original as possible. Award ribbons or prizes. Display the winning posters in the sanctuary and various places around the church.

CHILDREN'S SUNDAY BULLETIN COVER

Invite all the children in your Sunday school to submit an original drawing to be used on the bulletin for Children's Sunday. *(Clear this through proper channels.)* Provide sheets of paper, or specify the specific size of your regular bulletin front.

Select the best one and use it on the bulletin. You may wish to duplicate a few of the other drawings to be used as inserts. Or you could display them on a special bulletin board in the vestibule for everyone to enjoy.

COLUMBUS DAY

In Hawaii, October 12 is both Columbus Day and Discovery Day. They use this day to salute all the great discoveries of history. You may wish to expand your celebration of this day by honoring famous discoveries in your state or area.

COLUMBUS DAY MURAL

Let your pupils prepare a mural on which they chart Columbus' route. Then add drawings that show events at different points along the route. Have them select Bible verses that would have been particularly helpful to the travelers at various places along the way, or as they faced difficult obstacles.

COLUMBUS DAY PLATES

These plates, displayed on your classroom wall, will remind your pupils of the importance of this day. They will have studied the events of Columbus' trip and discoveries at school, so spend only a short time reviewing them.

Have each child select a favorite event he would like to illustrate. Have him draw it on a paper plate, using crayons or felt-tip markers.

BOOK WEEK
(Announced Week in November)

BOOK JACKET PUZZLES

If your church librarian has book jackets discarded from library books or book posters, see if she will let your pupils use them to make puzzles for the children's area of the library.

Glue the jackets to pieces of cardboard or poster board. Cover, front and back, with clear, adhesive plastic. Cut into puzzle pieces. Put all the pieces for one puzzle in a manila envelope with the title of the book printed on the front.

BOOK MOBILES

Ask your church librarian if your pupils could make special book mobiles to be displayed in the library during Children's Book Week. Collect enough of the newer children's books from her so that each child will have at least one to read. *(Good readers may wish to do more than one.)*

Have each child select a book to take home and read during the week. He is to bring the book back the next Sunday along with a wire coat hanger.

Cut a strip of brightly-colored poster board two inches wide and as long as the crossbar on the hanger. Punch one hole in the center of one of the long sides of the strip. Use yarn to tie it to the crossbar of the hanger. Print the book title on this strip.

Cut several squares, circles, or triangles from poster board. On each piece, write some information about the story, or draw pictures to illustrate different scenes. Information could include setting, names of main characters, major problems to be overcome, etc. Punch holes, evenly spaced, along the bottom of the title strip and at the top of each shape. Use lengths of yarn to tie each shape to the title strip. One shape should also include the name of the student and how he liked the book.

BOOKMARKS

Cut different colors of construction paper or poster board into 2 x 6 inch strips. Provide your pupils with a number of books of Bible facts or Bible quizzes. Have the children write an interesting fact from the Bible on each bookmark, or write a Bible question on one side of the bookmark and the answer on the back.

READING TICK-TACK-TOE

Go to your church library and borrow a variety of books on your pupil's reading level. Display them in your classroom.

To encourage pupils to start reading these books during Children's Book Week *(and to continue reading in the weeks ahead),* have them each prepare a tick-tack-toe grid on a nine-inch square sheet of construction paper. Use a ruler to mark off the lines to form a grid with nine three-inch squares.

Next, have pupils label each square with a category of books. *(You will have to determine the categories while in the library and prepare a list to share with the class.)* Possible categories are fiction, Bible stories, creation, animal stories, biography, etc.

Have pupils post their grids along the classroom wall or on a specially prepared bulletin board. Let pupils select books to take home and read. Each week they may write the names of the books they have read in the appropriate squares. First one to fill in three squares in a row is the winner.

All-Occasion Crafts

14

SPECIAL CRAFTS

Many of the following crafts can be adapted to use with any holiday or theme. The others are appropriate any time you need a special craft project for your class.

In the last section of this chapter, you will find a number of unusual art methods that will take your handwork times out of the ordinary.

GLASS-FOIL PAINTING

Have each child bring to class a piece of glass from an old picture frame, with the sharp edges taped. Have him trace around his piece of glass on a plain sheet of paper. Then have him draw a simple holiday *(or other)* design within the outline on the paper. Lay the glass over the design and boldly trace it on the glass with a permanent black marker. Discard the paper design. Turn the glass over and color in the design with bright-colored felt markers. *(Color the background around the design if you like.)*

Cut a piece of aluminum foil the same size as the glass. Crush the foil and then smooth it out again. Sandwich the foil between the glass *(with the black outline on the outside)* and a piece of cardboard cut to fit. Tape the three parts together with colored plastic or fabric tape. Attach a picture hanger to the back and hang it on the wall.

ROLL-ON PAINT PROJECT

If your pupils enjoy painting, but are bored with the usual paper and brush method, here's a new twist *(or roll)* they'll love.

Ask each pupil to bring to class a cardboard box, ranging in size from eight to fifteen inches *(shoe boxes work well)*. Provide shallow bowls of poster paint, plastic spoons, a quantity of marbles, and construction paper or poster board cut to fit the bottom of the boxes. Drop several marbles into each color of paint.

Have each pupil fit a sheet of paper in the bottom of his box, use a spoon to dip out one or two marbles, and drop them inside the box. The box is then tipped from side to side and back and forth as the marbles leave a design. Redip the same marbles, or use marbles from different colors of paint each time, and repeat until desired effect is achieved.

CIRCLE ART

This art project will call for lots of creativity on the part of your pupils, with very little cost.

Bring a supply of old magazines to class. Have pupils tear out a few pages of brightly-colored pictures or advertisements. Using a nickle as a pattern, have them draw a quantity of circles on the colored areas of the pictures and cut them out.

When each child has a number of circles, give him a sheet of construction paper for a background. Have him arrange the circles to make a picture of his own design. He may wish to make a border of circles around the edge of his paper, and then overlap several circles to outline animals or people, make trees, birds, fish, butterflies, etc. Some of the circles can be cut in half or quarters or trimmed to help shape the figures. Glue the circles in place.

Variation: Cut circles from different colors of construction paper, or use circles for main parts of picture only. Then complete it with crayons.

BIBLE WALL HANGING

Have each child select a favorite Bible verse and letter it neatly on a sheet of light-colored construction paper. Supply each one with a piece of felt or burlap cut large enough to leave a wide border around the Scripture sheet. The top and bottom edges should each be glued over a length of doweling, cut the same width as the piece of fabric. Attach a ribbon or piece of yarn to the top corners for hanging.

Carefully tear around the edges of the piece of construction paper *(with verse printed on it)* to give a more interesting effect. Glue the paper to the center of the hanging.

Variation: Instead of putting the verse on construction paper, let pupils cut out letters from different fabric and glue in place on the hanging.

GIANT STORYBOOK

Children who are already familiar with the Bible stories in your lessons will take renewed interest in reviewing them when they become a part of this oversized storybook.

Secure a large carton or appliance box from which to cut a cover *(make it about four feet high)*. Cut heavy paper for pages, perhaps having one page for each of the thirteen Sundays in a quarter. Put the book together with oversized book rings, so it will stand upright in a corner of your room.

Let pupils decorate the cover any way they wish or follow your suggestions. Each week, let the children draw a picture or summarize the story in some way. Add it to that page of the storybook. If you have a summary and picture of the day's story on a take-home paper, you could put that in the center of the page and encourage students to add original drawings, comments, or reactions.

BIBLE STORY MOSAIC

Before class, decide on a simple shape to represent a character or item important to the day's story, such as: an ark, giant, boat, whale, lion, etc. Draw the outline with pencil on a heavy cardboard or plywood background for each child. Cardboard should be painted with poster paint and plywood should be varnished first. This could be done by students the previous week.

Provide each child with a background and a quantity of plastic or ceramic tiles, available from a hobby store. Have him fill in the outline by gluing the tiles in place to form a mosaic design.

Variations: Use poster board for the background. Cut small squares of poster board in contrasting colors to use in place of the tiles. Use poster board "tiles" on backgrounds used above, and shellac the whole picture when completed.

HANGER MOBILES

These mobiles will add color and life to your classroom any time of the year. Vary the designs to fit the holiday or season.

Give each child a wire hanger and have him stretch it into a diamond shape by pulling down firmly at the center of the crossbar.

Have him use his hanger as a pattern to cut a piece of butcher paper or art paper in a diamond shape to fit his hanger. Use transparent tape to tape the paper to the hanger, securing all the way around the edges.

Next, have each one paint a picture or design on the paper *(with hook at the top)* with poster paints. Let dry. Mobiles can be hung from the ceiling or light fixtures. Hang two or three together by hooking each hanger to the one above it.

PUFFBALL ART

This project can be prepared in the classroom, but it will have to be baked in the church kitchen or taken home by the teacher to be baked and returned the following Sunday.

Adjust quantities according to the number of pupils. Mix one cup flour with three-fourths to one cup water *(per bag of cotton balls)* until smooth. Divide the solution between two or three small bowls. Color each with a different color of food coloring *(or omit the color and paint after baking).*

Have pupils drop cotton balls, one at a time, into the flour solution, swishing them around with their fingers to coat. Then, carefully, lift them out and position on a nonstick cookie sheet *(or prepare sheet with nonstick spray).* Do not squeeze balls. Use cotton balls to create the shape, animal, or design of their choice. Be sure the balls touch one another.

Bake for one hour in a 300° oven until hard. Uncolored balls can be painted. Mount finished figures on pieces of poster board, if desired.

SAND PAINTING

You will need clean, dry sand for these textured paintings. *(Put sand in cheesecloth. Run water through it until the water runs clear. Dry thoroughly.)*

Mix dry sand with small amounts of liquid poster paints to make a variety of different colors. Spread colored sand on sheets of newspaper to dry.

Box tops from shoe boxes, or the like, make good bases for the sand paintings. Paint the inside of the box lid and both sides of the lip with poster paint. Let dry. Have pupils draw a design or print a simple message such as "God Loves You" or "Jesus Loves Me" in block letters on the inside of the lid. Cover one section of the design or one letter with white glue. Sprinkle the glue with one color of sand. Shake the excess onto a cookie sheet to be reused. Repeat the same procedure for each different color until the painting is complete.

When the glue has dried, spray the finished picture with varnish or lacquer.

GEOMETRIC ART

These unusual creations are made from dried peas and round, wooden toothpicks. The dried peas will have to be soaked at least six hours before using to soften them. Softened peas will become the connectors between the pointed toothpicks. They will harden and hold tightly when they dry out in a day or two.

Give each pupil a generous supply of both peas and toothpicks. Let his imagination soar as he creates a building or other geometric shape. Let each one name his creation and then display it in the classroom.

CORRUGATED CARDBOARD ART

Let your pupils use this unique art form to make pictures of the day's Bible story. They should plan a simple outline scene on a sheet of scratch paper first. This idea works best with one or more large objects in the middle of the picture rather than a lot of detail.

Using dark, felt-tip pens or crayons, have the child draw his outline picture on a sheet of corrugated cardboard. *(Cut about 9 x 12 inches from the sides of cardboard boxes.)* The next step may require assistance, depending on the age of the pupils. With a single-edge razor blade, or mat knife, cut carefully along the inside of some of the main outlines of the picture. Cut through the top layer only. Tear away the top layer on those sections to expose the corrugated layer underneath.

Leave the corrugated sections natural. Use poster paint on the flat sections of cardboard around them.

RICE PAINTING

This project calls for rice in a variety of colors. To color rice, put raw rice in several baby-food jars. Fill each jar only half full. Add two or three drops of food coloring. Mix colors to make more choices if you like. Shake the jars until the color is evenly distributed on the rice. Pour it on waxed paper to dry.

Give each child a piece of poster board. Let him draw a simple object on it that is important to the day's lesson, such as an animal, ark or boat, cross, person, etc. Cut it

out. Next, have him spread glue on one section of his figure and cover it with one color of rice. Let dry slightly, and then blow away any excess rice. Repeat with each different color needed to complete the design. Display on a classroom wall or bulletin board.

ANCIENT TABLETS

A local carpenter's shop or building sight will probably be able to supply the bases for these replicas of ancient "stone tablets."

Each child will need a piece of plywood about 4 x 5 inches. If the edges are rough, provide sandpaper to smooth them off before proceeding.

Have available some clay in a variety of colors, if you like. Each child will then use his fingers to smooth a thick layer of clay over the surface of his board. When the board is covered, and the clay is smooth and evenly distributed, have the child use a nail to carefully "carve" the day's memory verse on his tablet. If he makes a mistake, it is easy to "erase" and redo.

These boards may be left in the classroom and a new verse written on them each week.

PEEP-BOX SCENES

Individual Styrofoam boxes that hamburgers come in make excellent holders for a Bible-story scene. Have children save these, or purchase the number you need from a local restaurant.

Provide each child with a different Bible-story picture that can be trimmed to fit inside the top of the box. Have him trim it and glue it in place *(provide patterns to use if needed)*.

Next, provide single-edge razor blades, or mat knives, to cut two-inch circles out of the center bottom of each box. Put glue around the edge of the box to glue it shut. Pass around "peep-boxes" for all to see.

Variations: Make several boxes to illustrate different scenes from one story. Pass the boxes around the class as you tell the story. *(If hamburger boxes are not available, use two foam meat trays. Put the picture on one, cut an oval hole in the center of the other, and glue the fronts together.)*

CLASSROOM WASTEBASKET

Involve your pupils in making your room look more attractive. An old metal wastebasket can be restored and provide a class art project at the same time.

If the basket is dented, straighten out the dents as much as possible. Bring a large supply of Bible-story pictures, like those cut from take-home papers.

Let pupils all cut out or trim pictures and glue them, like a collage, to cover the basket completely. Be sure all loose corners are glued down. They may also want to add Bible verses or captions cut from papers or elsewhere. When the glue is dry, coat the basket with clear shellac.

HOLIDAY PLAQUES

Each child will need a 4 x 7 inch rectangle of cardboard, about eighteen popsicle sticks, white glue, and holiday-colored yarn or cord. Coat one side of the cardboard with a heavy layer of glue. Cover with popsicle sticks laid side by side. Put under a heavy book to dry.

Glue a length of cord to the upper corners for a hanger. Decorate the front of the plaque with self-adhesive holiday stickers, 3-D holiday decorations, fall leaves, dried flowers, paper snowflakes covered with glitter, seashells, or anything else that depicts the holiday or season.

Display finished plaques in the classroom, or send them home as a decoration or gift.

HOLIDAY IN YARN

Draw a holiday or seasonal picture. A simple, line drawing is best. Work on only a small portion at a time and go over the lines with glue. Immediately press appropriate colors of yarn over the glue lines. Add more glue and yarn as needed to complete the picture. Some of the main sections can be filled in by continuing to swirl the yarn around until a section is covered.

MISCELLANEOUS METHODS

Following are a number of art methods that can be used to add variety to your handwork sessions. Adapt them for classroom use to suit your particular needs for holiday, seasonal, or everyday crafts.

Antique Drawing: Draw a picture with crayon on construction paper. Paint over the whole picture with white poster paint thinned with water.

Blind Drawing: Put point of pencil on paper, shut eyes, and draw a picture without opening eyes until finished.

Chalk Art: Wet construction paper with a sponge and draw on it with chalk dipped in a solution of one-half teaspoon sugar to one-half cup water. *(Provide a small paper cup of sugar water for each student.)*

Coffee-Filter Designs: Use dropper bottles of food coloring to drip different colors onto a wet coffee filter. Dry and mount if desired.

Crayon Pictures: Color a sheet of white construction paper completely with thick crayon in a light color. Color over that with a medium color, and then finish with a layer of heavy black crayon on top. Use a pinhead to scratch a picture on the sheet. Go through one layer for some parts and two layers for others.

Crayon Rubbings: Lay a sheet of thin paper on different textured surfaces. Rub with the side of a crayon to reveal the textures on the paper.

Crayon Shavings: Shave old crayons on a food grater. Use with glue to fill in different sections of a simple line drawing.

Finger Painting: Use unusual backgrounds, such as: foil, wood, newspaper, cellophane, foam meat trays, or burlap. Use new materials for the paint, such as: shaving cream, toothpaste, cooked squash, mashed potatoes, mud, pudding, cornmeal mush, tapioca, etc.

Foil Painting: Cement a sheet of foil to a piece of cardboard. Paint over the foil with black Tempera paint, covering it completely. When dry, scratch a picture in the black paint with a pinhead or nail.

Glue Ink: Distribute white glue among several small glue bottles. Add a few drops of different food colorings to each small bottle and mix well. Replace caps, open to adjust the flow, and use glue bottle like a "pen" to draw pictures and designs.

Graph Paper Pictures: Make pictures on graph paper by filling in the squares with crayon or felt-tip markers in a planned design.

Paper Tearing: Instead of cutting out figures, tear the shapes from construction paper.

Potato Printing: Cut a potato in half, crosswise, and sketch a pattern on one raw end. Use a knife to cut away the unwanted sections of the potato to leave just the design. Use a brush to cover the design area of the potato with thick poster paint. Stamp the surface of the paper. Repeat.

Roll-on Painting: Fill clean, roll-on deodorant bottles with poster paint. Replace ball, and use to paint pictures.

Sponge Painting: Draw pictures with sponges dipped in poster paint mixed with liquid detergent to the consistency of cream.

Squeeze-Bottle Printing: Fill squeeze bottles *(like those used for catsup or mustard)* with different colors of poster paint. Squeeze small amounts of different colors onto one side of a folded piece of construction paper. Refold paper over the paint and rub over the paper firmly. Unfold paper and let dry.

Stick Painting: Draw pictures by dipping different kinds of sticks and twigs in the poster paint. They are your natural brushes.

Straw Painting: Use a drinking straw to blow blobs of poster paint around on a sheet of paper.

String Painting: Dip a length of string in poster paint and use it to make designs on the paper. Repeat with a different color, using a new piece of string for each color.

Tissue Paper Pictures: Cut or tear different colors of tissue paper into shapes needed to form a picture. Glue them to a construction-paper background, overlapping the pieces. Add details with crayon.

Transparent Pictures: Cut or tear colored tissue paper into interesting shapes. Arrange them on a sheet of waxed paper. Cover the finished design with a second sheet of waxed paper. Carefully slip both sheets between newspaper. Iron with a medium-hot iron until wax melts and fuses the two sheets together.

Two-Handed Drawing: With a pencil or crayon in each hand at the same time, draw a design.

Wallpaper Drawings: Add crayon designs or pictures to pieces of wallpaper that have muted backgrounds. This makes them look like they are part of the design in the wallpaper.

Wallpaper 3-D Art: Wet the back of prepasted wallpaper pieces with a sponge. Then create 3-D pictures with scrap materials, such as: drinking straws, buttons, yarn, beads, sequins, trims, cotton balls, twigs, etc.

Waxed Paper Pictures: Scratch a picture on a sheet of waxed paper with a nail *(be careful not to tear paper)* and mount it on bright-colored construction paper.

Wet Tempera Art: Sprinkle different colors of powdered poster paint on sheets of manila paper that have been dipped in water. Blend the colors with a brush. Finish details with colored chalk.

All-Occasion Gifts

15

CARDS

HOLIDAY MOSAIC CARD

Your children can make interesting greeting cards for any holiday. Fold a 9 x 12 inch sheet of construction paper in half. On the front, legibly draw a simple holiday design *(pumpkin, heart, bell, etc.)* with pencil. Cut the colored sections of magazine pictures or advertisements into one-fourth inch squares. Cover one section of your design at a time with white glue and add the squares of colored pictures. Continue until the design is completely covered. Let dry and add an appropriate holiday greeting inside.

LOLLIPOP CARD

Glue a cellophane-wrapped lollipop to the inside of a construction paper card. Select a color of paper to fit the holiday. Purchase holiday-decorated suckers from a candy store if available.

Let pupils add leaves, stems, grass, etc. to make the lollipop into a flower. Add a holiday greeting to the front of the card and have the child sign his name under the lollipop.

COOKIE CUTTER CARDS

Collect metal cookie cutters in shapes appropriate to the holiday or season. Carefully put Mystic tape around the cutting edges of each. *(This will keep the children from getting cut on the edges.)*

Put poster paint in shallow pie pans and let pupils dip taped edge of cutter into paint. Stamp onto a 6 x 9 inch sheet of construction paper in an overlapping design. Use one or more colors or shapes on the card. When the paint dries, fold card in half and write a message inside.

Variation: Make gift wrap by stamping designs on tissue paper.

COLORING BOOK CARDS

For each card you will need a 9 x 12 inch sheet of construction paper folded in half. Supply a quantity of coloring book pages of simple objects. Let each pupil choose a page, color it, cut it out, and glue it to the front of his card. Print a verse on the inside that is appropriate to the holiday or occasion.

BATIK GREETING CARDS

Decide on an appropriate shape for the front of the cards, depending on the occasion, i.e., heart for Valentine Day, flower for Mother's Day, flag for July 4, car for Father's Day, etc. You may want to supply patterns or let older pupils draw their own designs. *(Do not let the younger children do any cutting. Do it for them.)*

For each card, fold a sheet of heavy paper in half and outline the shape on the paper. Be sure to put one edge of it on the fold *(at the top or left-hand side).* Do not cut it out yet.

Use crayons to fill in the details, but don't color it all. Next, paint over the crayon with a thin layer of poster paint, covering the front of the card completely. *(The crayon will show through the paint.)*

When paint is dry, cut out the card, leaving the fold intact. Add message inside.

HOLIDAY SPATTER CARD

Give each child half of a 9 x 12 inch sheet of construction paper in a holiday color. Have him fold it in half to form a card. For each one, provide a holiday shape cut from paper. Lay the shape on the front of the card and spatter it with white poster paint *(use toothbrushes and small pieces of screen).* Remove the paper shape when the paint is dry.

Have each child outline his shape with white glue and add glitter in an appropriate color. Shake off excess.

Write a greeting inside.

BOOKMARKS

CRAYON SHAVING BOOKMARK

You will need poster board and some old crayons. Let several pupils work together to scrape crayons *(with a paper clip)* onto a piece of poster board. When a piece is well covered with crayon, put a piece of plastic wrap over the top and a towel over that. Iron over the towel with an iron on medium setting until crayon melts.

Cool and then cut poster board into 1 1/2 x 6 inch strips for bookmarks. Punch a hole in one end of each strip. Knot a piece of yarn through the hole and fringe its ends.

ENVELOPE BOOKMARK

Cut a 3 1/2 x 6 1/2 inch envelope in half. Cut off the flaps. You will need one-half an envelope for each bookmark. The closed corner of the envelope will slip easily over the corner of a book page.

Decorate it with colorful holiday or everyday seals, small pictures of Jesus, Bible story pictures, or small magazine pictures. Cut these out and glue on.

CARD/RIBBON BOOKMARK

Collect old greeting cards and provide a twelve-inch length of ribbon for each child. Let each pupil select one or two cards and use a drinking glass to trace around the portion of the card he wishes to use. Cut a second circle in the same way. Fold the ribbon in half. Glue the two circles together with the folded edge of the ribbon between them.

MUSLIN BOOKMARK

Each child will need a 2 x 8 inch piece of unbleached muslin. Let him use a straight pin to pull out threads at each end of the material to make a one-fourth-inch fringe. Next, have him draw on a design with crayon and add the name or initials of the person who will receive the bookmark as a gift. Place the bookmark crayon side down on some newspaper. Cover with a paper towel and press with a hot iron to make the design permanent.

CROSS/BIBLE BOOKMARK

Supply patterns for a 2 x 3 inch cross. Have each pupil cut out two crosses. Give him a four and one-half-inch length of ribbon to glue between the crosses. Have the ends extending evenly at the top and bottom of the cross. Put under a heavy book to dry, and then cut a "V" shape at each end of the ribbon.

GIFTS

FIREPLACE CONES

Your pupils can be involved in a practical craft project that will result in a useful gift for parents, or shut-ins, or nursing homes with fireplaces.

Gather enough pinecones to provide 6-12 per child. Melt one or two pounds of wax or old candles. Add two to four cups of sawdust. Then add the following chemicals, one at a time *(adjust all amounts according to size of class):*

  1/2-1 cup salt
  1/2-1 cup Borax
  2-3 tablespoons copper chloride
  2-3 teaspoons lithium or strontium chloride
  2-4 tablespoons calcium chloride

Heat mixture, but avoid getting it too hot, as it will not adhere to cones. Let child dip his cones, using tongs, and coating them generously. Lay out on waxed paper to dry. Burning these in the fireplace will make pretty colored flames.

Note: The last three chemicals are available at school or chemical wholesalers. Be sure not to use nitrates or nitrites for they are explosive.

CLAY MAGNETS

Bread is used to make the clay for this useful gift. Have each child bring three slices of white bread to class. Remove the crusts. Lay the bread on a sheet of waxed paper and pour three tablespoons of white glue over it. Child will knead glue into the bread until it is like clay and has lost its stickiness. Add a tablespoon of poster paint and knead it into the bread until it is evenly colored.

Now, shape the clay into a small animal or design of your choice. Let it dry overnight at least. Add a small piece of magnetic tape *(available at craft or hobby stores)* to the back. These magnets can be used to hold notes on the refrigerator door or metal cabinets.

HOT-DISH HOLDER

This is a welcome gift for mother, grandmother, or women friends.

Each child will need a twenty-five-foot length of braided clothesline rope (three-sixteenths-inch diameter), straight pins, and white glue.

Make a tight circle with the rope to form the center of the holder. Use straight pins to hold it together as needed. Continue to wind the rope tightly, using pins to secure until the circle is at least eight inches in diameter. Turn the holder to the back and lay it on a sheet of waxed paper. Use a brush to spread the back generously with white glue. Dry thoroughly and repeat the application of glue if needed.

TURTLE PAPERWEIGHT

Have pupils bring a flat, oval rock about 2 x 2½ inches for the body of this turtle paperweight. From scraps of leather or brown felt, cut four legs 1 x 1½ inches, a two-inch head, and a two and one-half inch tail. Glue in place on the bottom of the rock. Cut an oval of felt to glue to the bottom of the rock to protect the desk. Cover the ends of the other pieces. Add two sequin eyes to the head.

SPONGE CUP FOR STAMPS

Any adult would appreciate this gift for his desk. For each cup, you will need the small half of a L'eggs hosiery container (a colored one if possible), a sponge, and a plastic curtain ring.

Turn the egg half upside down on top of the sponge and trace around it with a pencil. Cut out the circle, and then cut the rest of the sponge into small pieces. Put the pieces into the egg. Leave just enough room for the sponge circle to sit on top, flush with the rim on the egg half. Attach the plastic ring to the bottom of the egg with white glue so it will sit upright. The sponge can be dampened to moisten stamps. Eggs may be decorated with a couple of canceled stamps. (Soak stamps in water to loosen from envelope, dry, and glue to egg.)

CHEESECLOTH "PAINTINGS"

This process produces a very professional looking picture (with the look of an oil painting) that will be a welcome gift for all ages, depending on the choice of picture.

Collect a number of pictures. Old teaching pictures, calendar pictures, or any on medium to heavyweight paper can be used. Let pupils select a picture to suit the recipient, cut a piece of cardboard to fit, and glue the picture to the cardboard. Be sure to put the child's name on the back.

Next, cut a single-layer piece of cheesecloth slightly larger than the picture to be covered. When the glue has dried, spread the cheesecloth over the picture. Shellac it in place. Using a brush and starting in the center, smooth the cheesecloth out to the edges of the picture. Set aside to dry (overnight).

Repeat the shellac from one to three times, until desired effect is achieved. Wait at least a day between each coat, or add one coat each Sunday. A frame may be cut to size from cardboard and covered with wood-grained, self-adhesive paper. Tape picture to back of frame, and add a picture hanger at the top.

MOSAIC BOX

This could be a gift for anyone. Each pupil will need an empty cigar box or inexpensive school box. For several weeks ahead, have pupils save eggshells. (Wash and remove the membrane.)

Let the children break the shells into small pieces. Put different food colorings in individual paper cups (or use Easter egg dye). Divide the shells evenly between the colors, and put into the cups to soak. Spread out to dry.

Use a pencil and then a felt-tip marker to outline a design on the box. A simple, geometric design will be the easiest to use. Cover a small section of the design with glue and use tweezers to place pieces of colored shell on it. Cover each area of the design with a different color. Continue until the box is completely covered. Brush glue over the finished box, and let dry for at least twenty-four hours.

Finish the inside of the box by painting or lining it with felt. Glue a length of braid along the outer edges of the lid. Let the two loose ends cross and extend in the front for a handle. Finish the outside with clear shellac.

Variations: The same box can be made by

covering with seashells, small pieces of colored magazine pictures *(like a collage),* polished rocks, canceled stamps, etc.

TIE SNAKES

A class of older pupils can make these charming snakes as gifts for a children's home, a preschool class, or for younger brothers and sisters.

Have each pupil bring a discarded man's tie from home. *(You might pick up some extras at a rummage or garage sale.)* Also, collect a quantity of used nylon hose or panty hose. Let the pupils cut the legs into about four-inch pieces.

Have pupils stuff the ties with the pieces of hose and stitch the ends closed. This can be done by hand or on a sewing machine, if available. Securely sew on two buttons for eyes. *(If these are to be for very young children, glue on felt eyes.)* Add a "forked tongue" of red felt under the point at the wide end.

NUT CAN

Each pupil will need a pound coffee can with a plastic lid. Begin by covering the can with a piece of brown wrapping paper. Tape it in place. Next, glue over it a piece of burlap, cut to size, leaving one-fourth inch free at the top for the lid to fit. Around the bottom edge of the can, wind and glue four rows of heavy twine. Cover the lid with twine in a spiral design. Begin at the center of the lid and continue to wind it down to the lower edge of the lip.

Spell out "Nuts" with twine. Glue into place on the side of the can. Glue a filbert or other nut to the middle of the lid for a decoration.

PHOTO PAPERWEIGHT

This photo paperweight will make a perfect gift for parents or grandparents.

Give each pupil a clear furniture caster. Have him trim a school photo to fit the inside of it. Place the photo facedown inside the caster. Cut a piece of foil the same size, place it over the picture, and fill the hole with plaster of paris. Smooth off the plaster so it will sit level when turned over. After it dries completely, glue on a piece of felt cut to fit.

HOLIDAY CADDIES

Collect enough empty, covered containers *(coffee cans, shortening cans, mix cans, etc.)* for each class member. Cover cans with appropriate colored felt, and glue on holiday shapes and designs cut from felt. Add appropriate trims.

These caddies may be used to hold holiday treats.

LEATHER-FINISH GIFTS

The shape of the container selected will determine the gift made. Possible containers include dressing bottles *(for vases),* cans with lids *(for canisters),* empty soup cans or straight-sided jars *(for pencil holders).*

Have children bring a container from home or you may provide them. Give each child a container and a strip of masking tape in any width. Tear off small pieces of masking tape and cover the container in overlapping rows, starting at the bottom and working up.

When the container is completely covered, it can be colored with brown, wax shoe polish to resemble textured leather. Apply it sparingly with a small piece of rag. Wipe off excess polish with a clean rag.

Bible-Related Handwork

16

MEMORY IDEAS

MEMORY CHAIN

Provide a quantity of 1 x 6 inch strips cut from colored construction paper. Let pupils make a multi-colored paper chain by interlocking and gluing together about twelve strips. Write the day's memory verse on one of the strips for each child. Staple it to the end of the chain for a hanger. Let each child take his home and hang it on his bedroom wall.

Variation: Write a memory verse on each strip, one for each Sunday this quarter. When a child can recite a verse, he may add that strip to his chain.

BIBLE-MAZE GAME

Have each child bring to class a small, shallow box, or the lid to a box. Use the box as a pattern and cut a piece of cardboard to fit inside the box. On the cardboard, have him print the day's memory verse. Punch three or four holes in it. Put the cardboard inside the box. Place three or four small marbles or beans in the box. Cover it with a sheet of plastic wrap, securing it with tape underneath the box.

The child will learn the verse as he tilts the box to put all the marbles or beans into the holes at one time.

INDIAN HEADDRESS

Provide a pattern for pupils to trace around to make several colored, construction paper feathers, about six inches long. Each one will also need a headband. Make it four inches wide and long enough to go around his head with room to overlap the ends. Cut it from brown wrapping paper and fold in half lengthwise.

Give each child a list of memory verses to be learned during the coming weeks. Have him print one verse on each feather. As he learns a verse, he may glue that feather inside his headband. Let him wear the headband in class each Sunday. Let him add a feather each time he recites a new verse.

BIBLE STORY REVIEW

BIBLE STORY SHAPE BOOKS

The special shape of these books will add to the fun of reviewing Bible stories. Provide a number of patterns for different shapes that represent recently studied Bible stories, i.e., an ark, tent, comb, cross, animal, boat, etc. Let each pupil choose a favorite story and trace the shape on two pieces of poster board for a cover. On butcher paper make several pages to go inside.

Pupils may then add a title and a few details to complete the cover. Inside, let them write a simple account of that Bible story. Younger children can dictate their stories to a helper who will write it for them. Also, let them draw pictures to illustrate their story. Staple the book together at the top or on the left side. Or punch two holes on the left side and tie it together with a length of yarn or ribbon.

BIBLE STORY COMIC STRIPS

A recently studied Bible story, drawn as a comic strip, is a good review for your pupils. It can provide some interesting artwork to display in your classroom or in a church hallway.

Show some Sunday comics as a reminder to your pupils of how they are done. Have them draw the story scenes, each in a different frame, on a strip of butcher paper. Add a summarizing caption under each frame. Students may then take turns sharing their comic strips with the class. Display for others in the church to see.

PAPER BAG COSTUMES

Before acting out a Bible story in class, let your young pupils make these simple "costumes" from large, grocery bags. Before class, collect a number of paper bags so you have one for each child in class. On the front of each bag, draw a face and appropriate headdress for each character in the story. If you have more children than characters, make the extras into people in the crowd, animals, or even flowers in the field, etc.

Let the children color in your simple outlines. Then help them cut holes for eyes and larger holes at the sides for arms. You will have to slip the bags over their heads to see where to position the holes correctly.

When the bags are finished, let the children put on their costumes and act out the story.

BIBLE-RELATED HANDWORK

NUTSHELL BIBLE

Each child will need both halves of an unbroken walnut shell and a strip of paper, about 1 x 9 inches. Fold the paper, accordion-style, into one-half-inch segments. Start at the top and write one word of your memory verse on each segment. Write the reference at the bottom. *(The length of your strip can be adjusted according to the number of words in your verse.)* If you are not emphasizing any particular verse, Psalm 119:11 is especially appropriate and will fit on this length paper.

Use a small strip of adhesive tape as a hinge to hold the two halves of the walnut shell together. Tape the bottom of the verse strip inside one half of the shell and fold up the strip. Pupils may take their nutshell Bible with them and share the message with their family and friends.

BIBLE STORY GAME BOARD

Children love to play games. Preparing and playing their own Bible story game will help them remember important story facts.

Before starting on the game board, have them work together to make a list of facts about the life of a certain Bible character such as Paul (or facts in a particular Bible story). Next, they need to draw a winding path of boxes to cover a large sheet of poster board. In each box they will put a fact from their list. Every few spaces they will add an instruction to move forward or backwards a certain number of spaces, depending on the action involved. For example, "Shipwreck—go back two spaces," or "Survived shipwreck—skip one space," etc.

Let pupils decide on rules of play. Use the game as a presession or review activity.

BIBLE STORY BOOK JACKETS

Designing a "book jacket" for a favorite Bible story will help children learn all the basic facts you will want them to remember.

Bring in sample book jackets from home, or borrow them from the church library. Show them to your class, talk about what's included on them, and tell why.

Each pupil will then pick his favorite Bible story and prepare a book jacket to go with it. Give him a strip of butcher paper, about 9 x 20 inches. Have him fold it in half and then fold a three-inch flap on each end.

On the front, he will write the Bible story title or a more creative title of his own. Have him draw a picture to illustrate it. On the back, he might like to write quotes from his fellow classmates about how they like the story. On the front flap, he should write a brief summary of the story, continuing it on the back flap if necessary. At the bottom of the back flap, have him list himself as the "author" of this version. Let him give a brief life summary, like those on your sample book jackets.

Display the book jackets (opened out) on a classroom wall or bulletin board.

SAND TABLE SCENES

Involve your pupils in making sand table scenes when a Bible story lends itself to that kind of visualization.

If a regular sand table is not available, the scene can be prepared in a large, shallow box set on a table. Line the box with plastic before adding the sand.

Let pupils decide on a scene that will best depict the Bible story. Have them plan how to carry out the scene in the sand. Use a mirror for lakes, aluminum foil for rivers, and mound the sand to make mountains, hills, and valleys. Make people and animals from chenille wires. Make tents from burlap fabric, and shape buildings from cardboard or popsicle sticks. Pupils can use their imagination to complete the details of their scene.

READ AND PRAY CALENDAR

This special picture can be hung in a child's room to remind him to read his Bible and pray everyday.

Each one will need a 9 x 12 inch sheet of construction paper and four chenille wires. Show them how to make a stick person. Use one wire for the head and arms. Loop another through the first and twist to form the body and legs. Have each one make two stick figures and glue them to the sheet of paper, leaving the arms fee.

Cut a small black Bible from construction paper. Glue it between the hands of one figure. Bend the hands of the other figure and glue them together in a prayerful pose.

Pupils can finish their picture with any details desired. Since the stick figures are flexible, they may wish to seat the one with the Bible in a chair and put the other in a kneeling position. Do this before gluing them in place.

Across the top of the picture have each

one print, "Read Your Bible—Pray Everyday." Attach a small calendar to the bottom so he can circle the days that he reads his Bible and prays.

PAPER BAG KITE

This kite is easy to make, fun to fly, and helps the children share Jesus with their friends at the same time.

Give each child a lunch bag and have him draw a picture of the day's Bible story on one side, with the closed bottom of the bag at the top of his picture. Limit picture to the top half of the bag.

On the other side, write the day's memory verse, going only about half way down the side of the bag. Open up the bag and roll the free edge over twice to make a cuff. Punch a hole on each side of the bag, through the cuff. Tie a string to each side. Then tie the two ends of string together in the middle. Leave a long length of string to hang onto when flying the kite.

Add a tail to the kite by tying strips of cloth or crepe paper to a string tied to one side.

PAPER BAG CHURCH

Your pupils will enjoy making a paper bag church to take home as a reminder that they should be in God's house every Sunday. The only supplies needed are medium paper bags *(with square bottoms)* and poster paint or felt-tip markers.

Give each child a bag and have him cut the top edge off so it stands ten inches high. Next, he will fold the top down to make a cuff. Turn the bag upside down so the flat bottom becomes the roof of the church. Use poster paint or markers to make two, stained-glass windows on each side of the

church. Put your hand inside the bag and crease the bottom to form a peak on the roof.

Paint the roof, add a front door, draw steps on the cuff below the door, and paint another window on the back. Glue a cross to the top of the roof, if desired.

BIBLE LICENSE PLATES

Talk about how many state license plates reflect something about that particular state, including a logo, motto, or what the state is famous for.

Have pupils design a license plate for a favorite Bible character. The plate should feature the character's name across the center, the approximate date he lived in one corner, his hometown in another corner, and then a logo or motto that would reflect something for which the character is best known in the other corner. Put it on 6 x 12 inch poster board.

Let pupils share their finished license plates with the class.

VILLAGE SCENE

This handwork project will help remind your younger children of God's watchful care over all of us. Provide patterns for two or three different house shapes and one for a church with a steeple. Let the children cut a church from white construction paper and several houses from different colors of construction paper. Use crayons to add doors and windows.

Glue the church in the center of a 12 x 18 inch piece of light-color construction paper. Arrange the houses around the church. Draw a road from each house to the front door of the church. Add trees, flowers, hills, etc., to complete the picture. Across the top have them write, "God Cares for Us All."

Missions Crafts 17

MISSIONS SCRIPTURES

Here are a few Scripture references that could be used in connection with mission study, missionary conferences, or mission-related craft projects:

Isaiah 6:8, 9   Mark 16:15
Matthew 9:38   Luke 5:10
Matthew 25:40   John 3:16
Matthew 28:20   Acts 1:8

POSTER CONTEST

Involve your pupils in making original posters to advertise an upcoming missions convention. Give ribbons or awards for the winning entries. Display all posters around the church on bulletin boards or on easels set in strategic places. They could also be hung in the convention display area.

Note: Be sure to supply students with all nec-essary information they will need to com-plete their posters.

MISSIONS WALL HANGING

This small wall hanging will be a reminder to your younger students that Jesus loves all boys and girls, no matter what their color or where they may live.

Each child will need a piece of felt cut 2 x 8 inches, a gummed picture hanger, and some self-adhesive seals of Jesus and children of many lands.

Give each child a piece of felt. Have him lick the hanger and put it in place on the back of one two-inch end of the felt. Next, have him add the Jesus sticker at the top of his hanging. Finally, provide five or six heads of children of other lands. Have the pupils stagger them down the length of the strip. If time allows, give each foreign-child sticker an appropriate name. Talk about the country he represents.

Encourage students to put the wall hang-ing in their room at home.

MISSIONARY FLASH CARDS

Pupils can help prepare these flash cards, and then enjoy using them to play matching games.

Cut a quantity of cards from poster board, 4 x 6 inches is a good size. Divide your class into three or four groups to represent three or four different missionary families or countries you have been learning about. Each group will make a set of flash cards for its assigned family. On each card, they will write a fact, draw a picture, or glue on a magazine picture. The cards for each group could include: family name, picture and/or first name of each family member, name of country, picture of typical house, simple map outline of country, any pictures that represent the particular country, etc. When the cards are finished, they should be backed with two or three small squares of flannel or sandpaper so they will adhere to the flannel board.

Mix all the sets of cards together (reserving the family-name card from each set). One at a time, put up a family-name card at the top of the flannel board. Distribute the remaining cards among the class members. Let all the children, who think they have cards that belong to that group, come up and put their cards on the flannel board. Let pupils correct any mistakes. When each set is completed correctly, remove those cards and put up the next family-name card. Repeat the procedure for each set.

QUILT BLOCKS

Cutting out quilt blocks can be a special missionary project that your pupils can work on during a craft session. As an ongoing project, it can be worked on during presession or other free times.

Encourage pupils to bring in remnants of fabric that they collect from mothers, grandmothers, and interested friends or church people.

All blocks should be cut a uniform size.

The standard size post card is the most universal. Patterns cut from sandpaper won't slip and are easy to work with. Show children how to cut the blocks, making the best use of the material. Keep the pattern "square" with the weave of the fabric. If a variety of types of fabric are used, have someone sort them into like types, putting together the cottons, corduroys, flannels, polyester knits, etc.

Contact your missionary committee to find out where and how these quilt blocks can be used best.

Note: It is best to contact the committee before beginning such a project to find out specific needs and guidelines.

MISSIONARY MOBILES

Mobiles will bring your classroom to life while your pupils learn about the different missionary countries. Magazine pictures of the different countries will be most effective, but the pictures can also be drawn by the pupils.

For the mobiles, each child will need three pieces of string (about 6 inches long) and three pieces of poster board in different colors, a triangle, a circle, and a square (about six to eight inches in diameter).

Punch holes in the top and bottom of the triangle and the circle, and a hole in the top side of the square. Use the pieces of string to tie the shapes together, with the triangle at the top and the circle in the middle. A string at the top of the triangle can be used later to tie the mobile to the light fixture or ceiling.

Have pupils select or draw five pictures that depict life in the countries of their choice. These will be glued or drawn, one to each side of the shapes, with the name of the country (or missionary) printed on the sixth side.

Before hanging the mobile, let each child show his to the class, explain the pictures, and tell what he knows about the missionaries or country.

MISSIONS BUILDING

This idea can be adapted to the study of most any missionary country. Simply change the building to fit the country.

Have your pupils use a card table for the basic structure. Make it an Alaskan igloo *(cover it with a white sheet with ice blocks marked on with a black felt-tip marker),* African hut, Japanese pagoda, etc. The structure does not have to be fancy—loosely represent the kind of building common to that particular country.

Put a supply of books and magazines about the country outside the entrance. On the interior wall, tape up pictures of the missionary, mission letters, pictures of the country, etc.

Encourage pupils to use presession and free time to read the available material.

TRANSPORTATION POSTERS

It's important that we do all we can to help our pupils relate to missionaries as real people—to better understand what their lives are like on the mission field.

When a missionary visits your church is a good time for your class to ask questions. Or they can write to them on the mission field.

What they will need to know for this project is how the missionary travels from this country to his mission home, and then how he travels when he is in that country. Be sure to find out all the different modes of travel he may have to employ to get all the way to his station. Also, find out all the different kinds used within the country. For example, he may fly to the country, but then have to take a train, boat, ox cart, horse, or whatever to actually reach the mission station.

When this information has been obtained, your pupils can make a transportation poster for each missionary. On it they will draw or glue pictures of the different vehicles on an outline of the trip. Also include pictures of the different types of transportation.

MISSIONARY SCENES

Tabletop scenes made by your older pupils will be a welcome addition to a missions convention display area. Divide your class into work groups of three or four students each. Let each group select a country that will be recognized during the convention.

Provide a number of books and magazines that will give needed background information on each country. Have each group study their country together and decide on a scene that will best convey the life-style of that country. They will need to plan the scene and how they will construct it. Give as much guidance as needed, but encourage them to use their own imaginations.

Scenes should be constructed on a portable base. Then they can be moved from the classroom easily when needed for display.

Suggestions: Make people from chenille wire or clothespins with paper faces glued on *(faces can be cut from magazines or catalogs).* Use real fabric for clothing. With clay for a base make trees from chenille wire. Cardboard, craft sticks, or corrugated cardboard can be used to make buildings. Add sand, dirt, dried flowers, artificial grass, etc. to make the scene realistic.

BIBLE SCRAPBOOKS

These simple scrapbooks can be made by your pupils and sent to missionaries to be used in teaching the children in their countries.

Purchased scrapbooks with "magnetic" pages will make the books more durable, but pupils could make their own books with poster board covers and loose-leaf rings.

Before beginning, discuss with your pupils what kind of pictures should be included. It will be best to include only simple pictures and scenes, such as: a Bible, Jesus, sheep and shepherd, Christmas and Easter scenes, etc.

Let pupils select appropriate pictures, trim them neatly, and put them into the scrapbook without captions.

Variation: Older pupils could prepare flannel-graph figures or simple shapes cut from felt.

COUNTRY COLLAGE

Let each pupil in your class choose a country in which you support some missionaries. Have available old issues of travel magazines or *National Geographics.* Let each pupil select and cut out pictures of places and things that you would see in that country. When he has enough, the pictures can be glued to a sheet of poster board, collage style. Add the name of the country, cut from simple block letters, to a corner of the poster. These can be displayed around the church or in a display area.

MISSIONS PLACE MATS

If your church supports certain missionaries, make information about them available to your pupils. They can use it to make place mats as prayer reminders for use at home.

Find enough pictures, prayer cards *(or whatever your church makes available),* etc. so each child can have something about a missionary family. You may want to emphasize one particular family, or let each student select a family of his own choice.

Give each child a 12 x 18 inch sheet of bright construction paper. Have him write the name of the chosen family across the top. He can then glue on the family picture, draw an outline of the country where they serve, and label it with the country's name. He may also add pictures that depict that country, i.e., lion for Africa, pagoda for Japan, etc.

Finish the place mat by printing on it the words of a mission-related Scripture verse.

To protect the mat from spills, it should be covered front and back with clear plastic.

HUMAN-FAMILY COLLAGE

A discussion about missions is sure to include the differences between races of people. Our children need to understand that all people are the same in God's sight. Stress the ways in which all people are the same and share the same basic needs.

Preparing a human-family collage will help pupils see people of all races as belonging to one family. Have pupils go through travel magazines and *National Geographics* and cut out pictures of people who represent all different races. Have them glue all of them collage style to one large sheet of poster board. Add an appropriate caption in simple, black, block-style letters.

PRAYER POSTER

A personalized prayer poster is a good reminder to your pupils to pray for the people of other lands. It will help them to remember to pray for specific needs in countries where you have missionaries.

Each child will need a sheet of construction paper and a pattern for drawing a large *(six inch)* circle in the center of it. Before class, or in a brainstorming session with the group, decide on seven specific needs for which to pray during the coming week.

At the top of the poster print "I Am Praying." Next, decide on a picture, word, or symbol to represent each of the seven prayer needs. Write or draw each need, evenly spaced, around the edge of the circle. In the center of the circle, have each child paste a school photo of himself, glue on a sticker of a boy or girl *(to represent himself),* or draw a picture of himself.

He will take the poster home. Each day, as he prays for one need, he can draw a line with a crayon from the picture of himself to the need for which he has prayed. If he wishes to pray for the same needs on succeeding weeks, he may draw lines with different colored crayons each week.

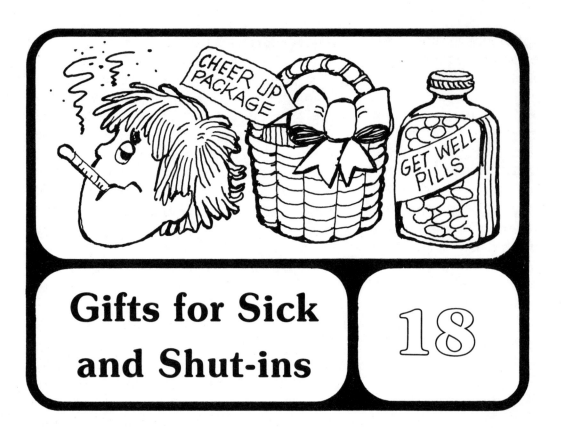

Gifts for Sick and Shut-ins

18

GET-WELL PUZZLE

Your pupils will enjoy making this special get-well card for a sick classmate. The sick child will get double pleasure as he reads the messages and then puts it together.

Cut a large sheet of white poster board into enough odd-shaped pieces so each child has one piece. Encourage each pupil to write a get-well message on his piece, sign his name, and decorate it any way he wishes, using crayons or markers.

Put the finished pieces in a manila envelope. Deliver it to the sick child with instructions to put the pieces together to form his get-well collage after he reads the comments from each of his friends.

Variation: Print a simple get-well message in the center of a twelve-inch square sheet of poster board. Have pupils sign their names around it. Cut square into puzzle pieces, put in an envelope, and deliver to the sick child.

FOR GOOD HEALTH

When one of the children in your class is sick, have the other pupils prepare a special "cheer up" gift for him.

Purchase a dozen *(or more if your class is larger),* large gelatin capsules from a drug store. Find a small box or pill bottle large enough to hold them all. Cut strips of typing paper *(one for each capsule)* four to six inches long and just wide enough to fit inside an empty capsule *(when rolled up).*

Let pupils have one or more strips on which to write personal notes, Scripture verses, original poems, or jokes. Roll up the strips and put one inside each capsule. Put all of them in the container and label it "Get-Well Pills. Take one after each meal. From your Sunday-school class."

FRIENDSHIP BOUQUET

This gift is appropriate for anyone who is sick or shut-in.

First, you will need to decide on a short

message of cheer for the sick person. Each word of your message will be on a separate flower in the bouquet, and each letter of the word will be on a separate petal on that flower.

Provide patterns for three-inch petals so pupils can cut enough of them, from crepe or tissue paper, to make each flower. With a marking pen, print one letter on each petal. Put all the letters for one word in a separate envelope and number the envelopes consecutively. Put these envelopes, assembly instructions, plastic straws for stems, and green florist tape to wrap stems all into a box. Wrap. Deliver to the sick or shut-in patient.

CHEER-UP PACKAGE

If you have a child in your class who will have to be in bed for an extended period of time, involve your pupils in preparing this gift package.

Have each pupil bring a small, appropriate gift from home (or provide them). Each one should wrap his gift and include a short note of cheer. Label each package with a day of the week, and put them all into a box or basket to be delivered to the shut-in.

BUSY BOOKS

Have pupils work together to prepare a "Busy Book" for a sick classmate.

Cut two 9 x 12 inch covers from poster board. Add several pages of typing paper, punch three holes, and hold together with loose-leaf book rings. (It will be easy to handle in bed.)

Gather together a stack of old Sunday-school take-home papers or children's magazines. Have pupils cut out jokes, puzzles, coloring pictures, activity and craft ideas, short stories, etc., to be pasted into the book. On one page at the front of the book write a get-well greeting. Have each child sign his name.

SICK "BUGS"

Have each pupil draw a picture of what he thinks the sick child's "flu bug," "cold bug," etc. looks like. Encourage them to make them as wild and fierce looking as possible. They may wish to name their "bugs."

Pupils should then write personal greetings and sign their names under their pictures. Deliver to the sick child to cheer him up.

"STICK MAN" CARDS

Give each child a 6 x 9 inch sheet of construction paper. Have him fold it in half to form a card. Also supply a stick of wrapped chewing gum for each card. Have the child glue it vertically to the front of the card and add a head, arms, legs, etc., to make a "stick man." Complete details as desired. Write a message inside the card.

GET-WELL GREETING BOOK

Collect a quantity of used get-well cards. Save only the front section from each. Punch a hole in the upper, left-hand corner of each card front. Keep these handy in your classroom.

When a pupil is sick, let the other children select a card, and write a message or comforting Scripture verse on the back. Collect the cards and tie them together through the corner hole with a length of ribbon or yarn. Makes a small "book" that a child can handle easily in bed.

SCRIBBLE CARDS

Prepare one large card on a 9 x 12 inch sheet of construction paper. Across the top write a get-well greeting. Use a dark crayon to make a large, scribble design over the rest of the paper.

Pass the sheet from pupil to pupil. Have

each one find an open section of the scribble where he can draw a face and then sign his name under it.

MYSTERY MESSAGES

A sick child will have fun assembling and reading mysterious messages from his classmates.

Give each child a 9 x 12 inch sheet of construction paper in a bright color. Give him eight 1 x 12 inch strips of construction paper in a contrasting color.

Have each one fold his 9 x 12 inch sheet of paper in half, lengthwise. Using rulers, mark the sheets and cut slashes one-inch apart, to within one-half-inch from each long cut edge *(cutting from the fold side)*.

Open out the sheet and lay it flat. Use cut strips to weave a mat by adding them to the 9 x 12 inch base. Have pupils print a message to the sick child by putting one letter in each square. Leave a blank square between words. Remove the strips, but first number them 1 through 8 on the end of each strip. Dismantle the mat. Clip the strips to the background sheet, or put each set into a flat paper bag.

Deliver to a sick child. Have him put each mat back together so he can read the message on it.

SOUP MATS

Mealtime will be more enjoyable for a sick person if your pupils make him special place mats to use at each meal.

Give each child a 9 x 12 inch sheet of construction paper. Let him draw a picture, write a Bible verse, poem, or personal note, and add a border of glitter. Or, he may prefer to cut a "fringe" border all the way around the edges. Be sure to have him sign his name to his place mat.

CRAFT STICK PUZZLES

A child in bed will enjoy working unique stick puzzles. Let each of your pupils make a different one.

Select a picture. Glue craft sticks to the back of it, side by side. When the glue dries, carefully cut between the sticks. Put all the sticks for one puzzle in a separate envelope, seal, and deliver.

HOLIDAY MOBILES

If you have a child sick on a holiday, let pupils make a holiday mobile to hang over the bed as a reminder that they miss him.

Using appropriate colors, cut a variety of holiday shapes from construction paper. Cut enough so that each child will have one. Encourage each pupil to decorate his shape the way he wishes, write a cheerful note on it, and sign his name. He can use both sides of the shape.

Punch a hole at the top of each finished shape. Tie a length of ribbon or yarn to each one. To form a mobile, tie or glue the other end to the crossbar of a wire hanger at different heights.

Food-Related Crafts

19

NO-COOK CANDIES/COOKIES

Here are a number of candy and cookie recipes that can be made in class without any cooking or baking required. Use them for holiday gifts or classroom refreshments. *(Be sure to have all children wash and rinse their hands well before starting any of these projects.)*

STUFFED DATES

Bring to class whole, pitted dates, fondant, walnut halves, and powdered sugar. Have children stuff each date with a piece of fondant, roll it in a saucer full of powdered sugar, set it on a piece of waxed paper, and top with a walnut half.

WALNUT DOTS

Let children take turns stirring and knead-ing together $2/3$ cup sweetened condensed milk, $4 1/2$ cups powdered sugar, $3/4$ teaspoon vanilla, and $1/8$ teaspoon salt. When it is smooth, divide it in half and color each half by kneading in red and green food coloring.

When evenly colored, divide candy among the pupils. Let them shape it into $3/4$ inch balls and top each ball with $1/4$ of a walnut, pressing firmly to flatten ball slightly.

PEANUT BUTTER CANDY

Children can take turns mixing the ingredi-ents, rolling the candy into balls, then enjoy-ing it together. Mix $1 1/4$ cup peanut butter, 1 cup corn syrup, and $1 1/4$ cup each of pow-dered milk and powdered sugar. Make one or more batches, depending on the size of your class.

CHOCOLATE CANDY BALLS

Mix together $1/2$ cup cocoa, $1 1/2$ cups powdered sugar, and $1/8$ teaspoon salt. Add 1 cup chopped walnuts, $1/2$ cup plus 1 tablespoon sweetened condensed milk, and 1 teaspoon vanilla. Let children mix it well.

Roll into one-inch balls, and then roll balls in a mixture of 1 tablespoon cocoa and 1 tablespoon powdered sugar. Chill. Keep tightly covered in the refrigerator if they are not to be eaten right away.

CEREAL COOKIES

Take turns stirring together $1/2$ cup white corn syrup and $1/2$ cup peanut butter. Gradually add 3–$3\frac{1}{2}$ cups of crispy rice cereal. Mix until thoroughly coated.

Spoon and pat into an eight-inch square, buttered pan. Cut in squares.

Variation: Let each child pat some of the cereal mixture into the bottom of a Styrofoam, hamburger box. If it is to be given as a gift, he can decorate the box with holiday stickers and tie with a ribbon.

SIMPLE FOOD PROJECTS

SUPER-SIMPLE IDEAS

Make pancakes in an electric fry pan. Let each child pour and turn his own.

Mix up frozen orange juice. For a variation, slice up bananas into small paper cups and pour orange juice over the top.

Have pupils spread a slice of bread with peanut butter and make a jelly face on it.

Make homemade ice cream in a cranking ice-cream maker. Take turns cranking.

Mix instant pudding with a hand beater. Take turns beating.

Make popcorn.

Make cinnamon and sugar toast. Spread hot toast with butter and then sprinkle it with a cinnamon and sugar mixture *(2 tablespoons sugar to 1 teaspoon cinnamon)*.

PEANUT BUTTER

Make peanut butter in a blender or food processor. Have pupils shell a large quantity of peanuts *(leave on the brown hulls)*. Put into machine and grind into butter. Add a small amount of oil. Mix well and add salt, if desired. Let pupils eat it on crackers.

CHURNING BUTTER

Make butter in a butter churn. Pour in cream and take turns working the dasher until the butter "comes." Pour off the buttermilk. Put butter in a bowl. Work and wash the butter, add salt, and shape into a cube. Let pupils try it on hot toast.

BUNNY SALAD

For each child, lay a canned pear half, cut side down, on a lettuce leaf. Cut a banana in half, lengthwise then crosswise, and dip in lemon juice to keep it from turning brown. Stand up two pieces of the banana on the small end of the pear to form ears. Make eyes and a mouth from whole cloves. Add a large marshmallow for a tail.

OPEN-FACED SANDWICHES

Peanut Butter, Apple, and Bacon: At home, fry bacon until crisp and cool. Bring to class along with apple, peanut butter, and bread. Let pupils grate the apple on a food grater and crumble the bacon. Mix peanut butter, apple, and bacon. Spread on slides of bread, cut into quarters, and eat.

Note: For each four open-faced sandwiches, you will need $1/2$ cup peanut butter, 3 slices of bacon, $1/4$ cup grated apple, and four slices of bread.

Peanut Butter and Banana: Mash banana, add peanut butter, and a little mayonnaise, Spread on bread, cut in quarters, and eat.

Note: For each four open-faced sandwiches, you will need 1 banana, ½ cup peanut butter, a little mayonnaise, and 4 slices of bread.

Peanut Butter and Nutty Honey: Mix peanut butter, chopped nuts, and honey. Spread on bread, cut in quarters, and eat.

Note: For each four open-faced sandwiches, you will need ½ cup peanut butter, 2 tablespoons chopped nuts, 2 tablespoons honey, and 4 slices of bread.

SNOW ICE CREAM

After a fresh snow, go outside and fill a large bowl with fresh, clean snow. Add milk, sugar, and vanilla to taste. Mix quickly before snow melts too much. Eat.

RUSSIAN TEA MIX

This tea mix makes a nice gift for any holiday or occasion. Put the ingredients into a covered plastic container. Take turns shaking the container until well mixed.

Pupils may then decorate a small baby food jar for each gift. Fill jar with tea mix. Be sure to include instructions for using tea *(and the recipe if you wish).*

For each batch, mix 2 cups Tang, 2 cups sugar, ½ cup *(heaping)* instant tea, 1 quart package of lemonade mix, ¾ teaspoon cloves, and ½ teaspoon cinnamon.

To drink, mix two heaping teaspoons of mix into a cup of boiling water.

TURTLE COOKIES

For these you will need a hot plate and one or more waffle irons *(as available).*

Melt 1 large bar of German cooking chocolate and 1 cup butter. Mix in 1½ cups sugar, 4 eggs, 1 teaspoon vanilla, ½ teaspoon salt, and 3 cups flour. Let children take turns mixing until well blended. Pour a small amount of batter onto each of the four sections of a waffle iron. Bake on medium heat until done *(about 1 minute).* Frost while still warm with powdered sugar. Can be eaten warm or cold.

STAINED-GLASS WINDOWS

This special candy can be made a week ahead to be sent home, given as a gift, or eaten in class.

Over a hot plate, melt together 3 squares of unsweetened chocolate and 2 tablespoons butter *(or margarine).* Let children add 1 beaten egg, 1 cup powdered sugar, 1 teaspoon vanilla, 1 cup chopped walnuts or pecans, and 1 package colored, miniature marshmallows. Stir until well mixed.

Sprinkle coconut on a sheet of waxed paper. Divide mixture in half. *(If class is small, divide equally among the pupils. Let each one make his own small roll.)* Make into two long rolls, about two and one-half inches in diameter. Roll in the coconut to cover evenly. Wrap in waxed paper and then in foil. Take home and put in the freezer until the next class session. While still frozen, cut into one-fourth-inch slices *(an electric knife works well)* to eat or give as gifts. Individual slices look like stained-glass windows.

SMILE COOKIES

Bring plain, round sugar cookies to class *(homemade or purchased).* Let pupils frost them with yellow frosting. With a cake decorating tube, add a smile face with chocolate frosting. These can be eaten in class or taken home and shared with a friend.

EGGNOG

Your pupils will enjoy making this special eggnog for a class party or when parents come to visit. Recipe makes enough for about twenty-five people.

Ingredients are: 6 eggs, ¼ teaspoon salt,

1 cup sugar, 2 teaspoons lemon juice, 1 can *(6 ounce)* frozen orange juice, 5 cups milk, and ½ teaspoon nutmeg.

Bring an egg separator to class. Let pupils separate the egg yolks from the whites. Put each into a two-quart bowl. Beat egg whites with a hand beater until frothy. Gradually add salt and one-half cup sugar, beating until stiff. Beat egg yolks until creamy. Gradually add one-half cup sugar while beating. Add lemon juice and frozen orange juice to egg-yolk mixture. Mix well, add milk, and blend. Pour egg-yolk mix into a punch bowl, fold in egg whites, and sprinkle with nutmeg.

PICTURE TOAST

This idea is well worth the extra effort of bringing a toaster to class. Make "paints" by mixing food coloring with small amounts of milk. Provide three or four different colors in small containers.

Give each child a piece of white bread. Supply a couple paint brushes *(clean)* with each color of "paint." Let child draw the design of his choice on the bread. Toast the picture bread in the toaster. *(It will make the picture very distinct.)* Provide butter and jam to spread on the toast before eating, if desired.

APPLE FACES

These decorated apple faces can be eaten in class or given as gifts. Give each child a nice, red apple. He will need broken toothpicks to stick the raisin eyes and nose on his apple, and to add a row of four miniature marshmallows for a mouth.

JIFFY FRUITS AND VEGIES

Peanut-Apple Faces — Let children spread apple slices with peanut butter and make faces on them with raisins.

Celery Cars — Cut celery sticks into three-inch lengths. Give one piece to each child. Fill with cream cheese, peanut butter, or a flavored cheesespread. Put carrot rounds on toothpicks. Add to the car for a steering wheel and tires. Raisins can then be stuck into the cheese for passengers.

Fruit and Vegetable Kabobs — Cut a variety of fruits and vegetables into bite-sized pieces. Let pupils pick the ones they like and put on toothpicks, layered with cubes of cheese.

CRACKER HORS D'OEUVRES

Spread round crackers with peanut butter and "decorate" them with miniature marshmallows, raisins, and small apple wedges. Children might like to serve these for a class party or when parents visit the classroom.

COOKOUT CRAFTS/FOODS

HOT DOG SKEWER

Each child can make his own hot dog/marshmallow skewer in class ahead of time. Have each one bring a metal coat hanger and three large, empty thread spools from home. *(You might have to help supply the spools.)*

Use metal cutters to cut the hook and neck off the hanger. Have pupils straighten out the hanger and then bend over a six-inch piece on one end *(Don't pinch the crease too tightly.)* and hold in place. Slip the three spools over the double section of wire and let go. The tension of the wire trying to unbend will hold the spools in place.

Provide small pieces of sandpaper so each one can sand the paint off the point end of his skewer.

FOIL CUP

From household foil, make a disposable

cup for drinks. Give each child a twelve-inch square piece of foil (or as large as your foil is wide). Have him fold it in quarters. Then fold in half diagonally to form a triangle. With the diagonal fold at the bottom, bend the two side points up alongside the top point. Fold down the tips to anchor and open out the cup.

FOIL DOGS

Give each child one or more hot dogs. Slit each one open, put a strip of cheese in the slit, lightly butter the outside, and wrap it in foil.

Cook in hot coals for three or four minutes and serve on a bun.

EGG ON A STICK

Very carefully tap a small hole in each end of a raw egg. Gently push it onto a thin stick or skewer. Hold it over the fire and cook to desired doneness.

BAKED BANANA SPLIT

Lay an unpeeled banana on a piece of foil (large enough to wrap it in). Make a slit in the banana, lengthwise through the skin but not all the way to the bottom. Fill the slit with chocolate chips, marshmallow creme, and chopped peanuts. Wrap it tightly in the foil. Cook over coals about five minutes. Open carefully, and eat it out of its skin with a spoon.

S'MORES

Roast one or two marshmallows on a skewer. Put four squares of a chocolate bar on one square of graham cracker. Lay hot marshmallows on top. Cover with a second graham cracker square. (Be prepared for seconds.)

Variation: For peanut-butter s'mores, prepare the same way, except spread the cracker with peanut butter instead of candy.

LEMON/GRAHAM PUDDING

Mix the juice of one lemon with a can of sweetened condensed milk. Add about one cup of broken-up graham crackers. Pour into pudding dishes and serve.

DOGS ON A STICK

Make light slashes along each side of a hot dog to bring out the flavor. Cook it over the fire on a skewer.

Wrap each hot dog in a strip of bacon, held in place with toothpicks. Cook over open fire until bacon is crisp and weiner is hot through.

Wrap the hot dog in biscuit or crescent-roll dough. Cook over an open fire on a skewer until dough is cooked and dog is hot.

POCKET STEW

Give each child a twelve-inch square of heavy aluminum foil. Into its center, have him break up small pieces of raw hamburger. To that add slices of potato, carrot, and onion. Season to taste with salt and pepper. Wrap securely in the foil, and cook over hot coals until done. Cooking time will vary, depending on hotness of the fire, etc. Check periodically for doneness. Stew can be eaten out of foil.

CHEESE BREAD

Slice a loaf of french bread into one-inch slices. (Being careful not to cut through the bottom crust.) Mix grated cheddar cheese with butter and season as desired. Spread it between slices of bread, wrap in foil, and heat over hot coals until bread is hot and cheese is melted.

Major Craft Project

20

CHURCH MADE OF SWEETS

This project will be appropriate when you are learning about any aspect of the church.

For a base, use a large shoe box with cardboard peaks taped to the front and back (narrow ends). Cut a roof from cardboard, being sure to allow for a little overhang all the way around. Fold the roof down the center. Glue it in place on top of the church. Add a milk-carton tower to the top if you like.

Let the children cover the church with candy, cookies, and marshmallows, using frosting for glue. Cover the roof with candy wafers. Two chocolate, sugar wafers (cookies) make a good door, and brightly-colored candies will make stained-glass windows. Cover the remainder of the building with even rows of miniature marshmallows. If desired, mount the church on a large piece of cardboard. Make a yard around the church by using candy, cookies, and marshmallows to make grass, paths, flowers, etc.

ROUND PLAQUES

These attractive plaques can be made in a variety of sizes, depending on the size of lid selected.

Each child will need a plastic lid from a container such as potato chips, peanuts, whipped topping, margarine, coffee, shortening, etc. Have him outline his lid, both on a piece of cardboard and on a piece of felt or burlap. Glue the circle of fabric to the cardboard.

Next, cut the center portion from the plastic lid and discard it. Save the outer rim for a frame. Cover the rim by wrapping it in yarn of a contrasting color. You may need to use a little glue to hold the yarn in place while wrapping. Glue ends of yarn on the back to secure. Glue the frame in place on the fabric-covered circle.

Complete the plaques by cutting out designs from felt and gluing them in place within the frame. Designs could correlate with the season. Attach a yarn or ribbon hanger to the back.

STRINGBOARD PAINTING

This unusual painting process will produce a unique plaque. It can be given as a gift or kept by the child to hang in his room.

Give each child an 8 x 10 inch piece of wood or fiberboard and about a four-foot length of twine. Sand all rough edges from the board. Paint the background in a solid color, or make irregular strips of two or three different colors. Let dry.

Next, wrap the board with the twine to form a "spider web" of crisscrossed strings. Tie securely in the back. If necessary, tape the strings in place on the back.

Put several colors of paint in squeeze bottles like those used for catsup or mustard. The paint should be thin enough so it will run *(but not too thin)*. Squeeze one color of the paint over the strings. Let it follow the strings to create an interesting pattern, tilting the board to make it run in different directions. Let this paint dry slightly before repeating with a different color. Repeat as desired, but don't let the paints mix together too much.

Let dry and then cover with one or two coats of varnish or shellac. *(Add a frame if you wish.)*

CRAFT STICK ALBUM

Pupils can make this special cover for an autograph book, photo album, diary, or the like.

Give each child a sheet of waxed paper on which to work and twenty-four craft sticks. Using white glue, put the glue along the edges of eleven sticks, laying them side by side to form the front cover of the book. Repeat with eleven more sticks for the back cover. To reinforce, glue a stick vertically across each horizontal end of both pieces. *(These will be on the inside of the covers.)*

Drill two holes on the left-hand side of each cover. Drill through the vertical stick on the third stick from the top and the third stick from the bottom. Cut several sheets of paper

to fit. Punch holes to correspond with the holes in the cover. Tie book together with a length of elastic cord. Decorate the front with permanent felt-tip markers, and then shellac if desired.

Note: Books could also be used for memory work.

CLAY – BEAD NECKLACES

Give each child some modeling clay, purchased or homemade. Have him roll the clay into long "snakes" about one-half-inch thick. Cut each strip into individual beads. They can be left in that shape, or rounded, if desired. Use a toothpick to make a hole through the center of each bead.

Bake beads in a 400° oven until hard. After baking, paint beads in a variety of colors *(or all one color)*. String on heavy thread or cord with a darning needle. Tie ends together and slip over the head to wear.

SET OF PLACE MATS

These plastic-covered place mats can be made as a gift, or be used by the children in a classroom or institutional situation.

Each place mat will be made from a 12 x 18 inch sheet of poster board in a pretty color. *(Let the children make one for each member of their family, a set of four for a gift, or one for themselves to use in class.)* Provide clear adhesive plastic and adhesive plastic in a solid color or print that contrasts with the color of the poster board. Cut a piece of the colored or printed plastic slightly larger than the piece of poster board. Apply it to the back.

Supply patterns for a variety of simple four-or-five inch shapes, such as: leaves, crosses, praying hands, animals, flowers, etc. Have the children trace the shape of their choice onto the backing paper of the plain or print plastic *(one shape for each mat)*. Cut out. Remove the backing paper and place the shape in the upper right-hand corner of the front of each mat. If desired, Scripture verses on strips of paper or gummed stickers can be put in the lower left-hand corner. Cover the front with the clear adhesive plastic. Trim the edges evenly.

PAPIER-MACHE BANK

These interesting banks are made with balloons of different shapes as a base.

Bring balloons in a variety of shapes to class. Let each child pick one to fit the shape of the bank he wishes to make—a pig, man's head, animal, etc.

Mix a batch of papier-mache, or use the purchased kind. Have each pupil blow up his balloon and tie the end securely. Cover the balloon completely and evenly with the papier mache, one-fourth-inch thick or thicker. When the covering is partly dry, add legs, tail, pig snout, ears, etc., to complete the figures.

It will take several days for the banks to dry completely. Paint the dried figure with watercolor paints and let dry. Cut a slot in the top for the money with a single-edged razor blade.

METAL COLLAGE

For these unusual plaques, each pupil will need a piece of plywood (any size) and a variety of shiny hardware, such as: nails, screws, nuts and bolts, drapery hooks, hinges, staples, etc. Encourage pupils to collect suitable hardware from fathers, neighbors, friends, or church members.

If possible, work outside. If you must work inside, protect the tables and floor with newspapers or plastic drop cloths. Protect the children's clothing. (Plastic trash bags with openings cut for the head and arms work well.)

Have each child preplan his design by arranging his selection of hardware on a sheet of paper to form an animal, design, or scene of his choice. When he has decided on a

design, have him paint his plywood with a thick coat of dark household paint. While paint is still wet, he can transfer his design to the plywood, placing each piece of hardware carefully on the painted surface. When the paint has dried thoroughly, the hardware will be "glued" tightly. Attach a hanger to the back of the plaque.

STORY CUSHIONS

Preschoolers or Primaries can make these cushions to sit on in class during story time. Older pupils can make them as a gift for younger classes.

Each child will need a large grocery bag, with the bottom cut out, and a stack of ten folded newspapers. Have him decorate both sides of the grocery bag with crayons or felt-tip markers. Then slip the stack of newspapers inside the decorated bag. Staple both ends of the bag shut. Cover the staples with colored plastic tape or masking tape.

CLASSROOM PILLOW

Involve your pupils in making a large, comfortable pillow for your reading center or a corner of your classroom.

Each child will need to bring to class a needle and thread and remnants of fabric. Provide patterns and have pupils cut the fabric into three-inch squares. You will need 288 squares in all. Next, have them make a strip by sewing twelve squares together, end to end. Show them how to put right sides together and baste a one-half inch seam between the squares. You will need twelve strips of twelve squares each for both the front and the back (twenty-four strips). When these strips are all basted together, you or a pupil's mother can stitch over the pupils' basting with a sewing machine. Press seams open.

Let the pupils take turns basting the twelve strips, side by side, in one-half inch seams. Repeat with the other twelve strips for the back. Stitch on the sewing machine and press seams open. Put the two finished pieces together, right sides facing, and have pupils take turns basting the outside edges together. Leave an opening on the fourth side for stuffing. Stitch outside edges *(leaving the opening),* turn right side out, and press.

Have children stuff the pillow with old nylons. Then sew the opening closed by hand.

THEME PICTURE PLAQUES

This attractive wall hanging can be made as a gift or for the child to hang in his room. For each one you will need a piece of one-fourth-inch plywood, about 18 x 24 inches *(or smaller if desired).*

Have each child sand the edges of his plywood smooth. Next, he will need to decide on a theme for the plaque, related to his own interests or the interests of the gift recipient. Some possible themes include: dogs, cats, birds, fish, butterflies, animals, sports, one specific sport, flowers, churches, Bibles, Jesus, Scripture verses, etc. These pictures could be supplied from a picture file, or have students go through old magazines and cut out pictures on their themes. They will need to cut carefully around each figure. Position the cut-out figures in a pleasing arrangement on the plywood. *(Do not cover completely.)* Glue the pictures in place and dry overnight under a weight.

Varnish over the plywood and pictures with a clear varnish. Let dry for several days. Make a border by nailing a length of one-fourth to three-eight-inch rope around the outside edge. Use thin nails with small heads.

SCRIMSHAW MEDALLIONS

Scrimshaw is the form of art done by whalers when they carve beautiful designs on pieces of ivory. Your class can duplicate this art form by using plaster of paris instead of ivory.

Mix up a batch of plaster of paris. Drop spoonfuls onto a sheet of waxed paper—one per child. After it begins to harden *(It hardens quickly.),* use a nail to make a hole at the top. Let dry completely for about ten minutes.

Give one medallion to each child. Have him use a nail or the head of a straight pin to etch a design on the front. The design can be a religious symbol, seasonal or holiday shape, or whatever he desires. Paint or shellac the medallion, and let dry. Thread a leather thong or cord through the hole and wear it around the neck.

BEESWAX YARN PAINTING

This process simulates the yarn painting done in Mexico. You will need to purchase sheets of beeswax at a hobby store. *(Sheets 8 x 16 inches are available for about 50¢.)* Give each child an 8 x 8 inch piece of plywood and a sheet of beeswax the same size.

Lay the beeswax on top of the plywood, set it out in the sun until the beeswax softens, and press the wax firmly onto the plywood. While the wax is warming, have the pupils sketch a holiday, seasonal, or religious design on an 8 x 8 inch sheet of paper. A simple, open design is best.

When the wax is soft, move to a cool place and use a large nail to scratch the planned design in the wax. Put wax back out in the hot sun to resoften.

Supply *(or have children bring)* a quantity of yarn in a variety of bright colors. When the wax is soft *(but not melted),* start pressing yarn into the wax. Start at the outside edges of each section of the marked design and winding it toward the center. Larger sections can be filled with several smaller swirled sections instead of one large swirl. Use different colors of yarn to emphasize each different section of your design.

Note: Be sure to move in and out of the sun as needed to keep the beeswax at the proper softness. If it gets too hot, the melted wax will soak into the yarn.

GENERAL ALPHABETICAL INDEX

TOPICAL INDEX

CRAFT SUPPLY INDEX